SUNDAY HOMILIES

SUNDAY HOMILIES

Liturgical Year A

William Bergen, SJ

Paulist Press

New York / Mahwah, NJ

Executive editor: Michael Gerstner

Cover image by Bradhostetler/Wikimedia Commons; background image by Livioandronico2013/Wikimedia Commons
Cover design by Michael Gerstner
Book design by Lynn Else

This book is set in Century Old Style.

Library of Congress Control Number: 2025949398

ISBN 978-0-8091-5836-2 (paperback)
ISBN 978-0-8091-8999-1 (ebook)

Published by Paulist Press
997 Macarthur Boulevard
Mahwah, NJ 07430
www.paulistpress.com

Printed and bound in the
United States of America

CONTENTS

Contents

Contents

INTRODUCTION

This Sunday Homilies series is a three-volume collection of reflections on the Sunday Scripture readings for each week of the liturgical year—Years A, B, and C. The homilies were selected from more than forty years of my ministry spent preaching at St. Ignatius Church, Baltimore, and St. Ignatius Loyola Church, New York.

HOW TO USE THIS SERIES

Whether used for personal reflection or as a companion to Sunday Mass, the books are organized to follow along easily with the Church's readings. The homilies align with the Sundays of the Lectionary,[1] so readers can simply find the associated Sunday and read that homily. The United States Conference of Catholic Bishops offers the daily readings slate and a full calendar at its website, which is an excellent resource for locating the Scripture readings for Mass. This is located at https://bible.usccb.org.

Each volume of this series corresponds to one of the three years of the Sunday Lectionary cycle—Years A, B, and C. Homilies are arranged by the liturgical seasons—Advent, Christmas, Lent, Easter, and Ordinary Time—rather than chronologically. This organization allows the books to remain easily useful year-after-year regardless of the shifts in the liturgical calendar.

---

1. *Lectionary for Mass for Use in the Dioceses of the United States, second typical edition,* Copyright © 2001, 1998, 1997, 1986, 1970, Confraternity of Christian Doctrine, Inc., Washington, DC.

Each homily in this collection includes references to that day's assigned Scripture selections from the Lectionary.[2] So, readers can also look up these passages in their Bible.[3] These are the same Scripture passages that appear in the Sunday Missal.

THE LECTIONARY AND LITURGICAL CALENDAR

The Lectionary is the Church's collection of Scripture readings for Mass. There are separate Lectionary cycles for weekdays and Sundays; this series is focused on Sunday readings. The Sunday Lectionary follows a three-year cycle, which rotates every fourth year:

Year A: Gospel of Matthew
Year B: Gospel of Mark (with selections from John)
Year C: Gospel of Luke
The Gospel of John also appears during Lent and Easter in all three cycles.

The liturgical calendar, which varies year-to-year, arranges the Lectionary readings around the particular dates in the calendar. The liturgical year begins on the first Sunday of Advent. So, for example, the 2025 liturgical year begins on the first Sunday of Advent in 2024. After Advent, the liturgical calendar proceeds through Christmas, Ordinary Time, Lent, Easter and then Ordinary Time resumes after Pentecost. (The number of weeks before and after Easter varies depending on when Easter occurs on the liturgical calendar each year.)[4]

---

2. Since May 19, 2002, the only English-language Lectionary based on the New American Bible is used at Mass in the dioceses of the United States (as per USCCB).

3. The New American Bible is conveniently available for any reader online at https://www.usccb.org/offices/new-american-bible/books-bible.

4. Detailed descriptions of the Lectionary and liturgical calendar from the United States Conference of Catholic Bishops form the basis for this discussion and are found at:https://www.usccb.org/offices/new-american-bible/liturgy; https://www.usccb.org/committees/divine-worship/liturgical-calendar; and https://www.usccb.org/faq/questions-about-lectionary.

Because of these organizing principles, the homilies in this series are ordered by the seasons of the liturgical year—rather than strict chronological order—so readers can efficiently plot a course through the changes that occur in the liturgical calendar from year-to-year.

THE COLLECTION

This collection was not written with publication in mind. So, on a few rare occasions, some Sundays were not included in this collection. When this is the case, I have noted for that Sunday: "Not included in this collection."

The homilies are presented essentially as I delivered them at the Mass.

In addition to the Sunday homilies, you will find a few supplemental homilies included in each volume. These homilies are applicable across all three Lectionary cycles:

Volume A: "Solemnities and Feasts that May Displace Ordinary Time Sundays." These feast days occur on fixed dates and do not always land on a Sunday. When they do, they take precedence over the usual readings in Ordinary Time. For when this happens, I have provided a homily in this volume.

Volume B: "The Easter Triduum." The three days of Holy Thursday, Good Friday, and the Easter Vigil comprise the Easter Triduum and are the most solemn days of the liturgical year. So, even though they are not Sundays, I have included homilies for these three Masses in this volume.

Volume C: "Holy Days of Obligation." There are four additional Holy Days of Obligation that do not appear in the regular Sunday contents of the three volumes, so I have included homilies for them here.

SEASON OF ADVENT

FIRST SUNDAY
OF ADVENT

First Reading: Isaiah 2:1–5
Responsorial Psalm: 122
Second Reading: Romans 13:11–14
Gospel: Matthew 24:37–44

❧

Advent is often described as a season of anticipation. The media will be full of cheerful warnings that Santa is coming and children need to be good. I remember being told as children that if we saw the curtains moving on the windows it was Santa watching us!

Most of us are probably anticipating family gatherings and holiday parties during the next month, and dreading city traffic jams and the frantic last-minute shopping. This year the usual anxieties are complicated by the stresses of our continued military involvement in the Middle East, the growing divide between the rich and the poor, and our dysfunctional Congress.

Scripture has its own anticipation over the next four weeks. The one constant message we'll be hearing is this: "The Lord is Coming! The Lord is Coming!" This is the promise that resounds through a thousand years of Hebrew Scriptures, a promise Christians believe has been fulfilled with the birth of Christ. Yet every Advent there's the continual exhortation to "be prepared" and to "stay awake."

What's going on here? Are we playing some sort of "make believe" game in Advent? Are we supposed to pretend that the Lord has not come as we prepare for Christmas? Surely not! The Lord has come, and the Church asks us to look back with amazement and gratitude for that First Coming, for the birth of Christ, and at the same time to look ahead with confidence to when Christ will come again as we say in the Creed every Sunday: "He will come again in glory to judge the living and the dead, and his kingdom will have no end." And that coming, the Final Coming, will be at some future time that no one knows. Only God knows! And so far, God hasn't told anyone!

I think the real importance of Advent is to get us thinking about the coming of Christ to us now! Right here! Today. This week. This month.

Christ is here with us today in the sacrament—the Eucharist, which we affirm is his real presence. Real food for our nourishment. Also, he's equally real, and just as truly present, in the Word. The Word of Scripture actually does announce him and presents him as Jesus the teacher—once again—for our time, now. "Your word is a lamp for my feet, a light for my path," says the psalmist (Psalm 119:105).

Also, Jesus is present in the neighbor! And as I'm sure you've told your children, the neighbor means more than the people next door! Jesus is especially present in the neighbor who is hungry. The neighbor who is homeless. Who is sick. Who is loveless or lonely. St. John tells us that God is wherever love is—whether it's love that's given, or love that's received.

And there's one more place to mention. Jesus is within you! We may call a church building God's House, and I frequently hear the teachers remind our grammar school children of this, as they lead them into church for Mass and other religious services. But each of us is really a house of God—what St. Paul calls "a Temple of the Holy Spirit" (1 Corinthians 6:19)—and God dwells within you!

We've come to know that it's in God's nature to come to us! In fact, God can be defined this way: as The One Who Comes To

4

Us! This can be the way I image God for myself, as The One Who Comes To Me!

And so, I see this as the great value of Advent. Advent reminds us that Christ comes to us now, in the ordinary workings of our life. The trouble is we can be so terribly preoccupied, and so easily distracted, that we pay no attention. We fail to notice the comings of Jesus to us in the here and now. A kind of sleepiness or spiritual laziness can overtake us, and we're not aware that God is quietly but continually acting in our lives.

One of the great modern teachers on the spiritual life, Anthony de Mello, a Jesuit from India, used to say that spirituality is about waking up, about becoming aware! This sounds like St. Matthew in our Gospel reading today: "Jesus said to his disciples: …stay awake! For you do not know on which day your Lord will come." He continues, "You also must be prepared, for at an hour you do not expect, the Son of Man will come."

We'll hear this call to watchfulness many times in Advent! Because the whole season is based on the conviction that the God who once came among us in the Incarnation continues to be present to us still.

For God is God of the present! There's no point seeking God in the past, or in the future. We don't need to look somewhere else, or to some other time. God is always in the present tense. This means, for example, instead of saying God watches over us, it is more accurate to say God is watching over us, now! Because our life is lived in the present tense. And a God who is God of the present doesn't easily go away. And is not easily dissolved into a warm memory, or a frightening future. A God of the present is to be encountered now— during this Advent! And if I'm really alert, I'll discover that.

SECOND SUNDAY OF ADVENT

First Reading: Isaiah 11:1–10
Responsorial Psalm: 72
Second Reading: Romans 15:4–9
Gospel: Matthew 3:1–12

Today we get to meet John the Baptist for the first time in Advent. He is the dominant figure in Advent, even more than Mary the mother of Jesus. And so, we'll be hearing more about John in the next few weeks.

He was a cousin to Jesus, as you know, and in many ways, they were alike! Both preached a message about the coming of a new age. And because of this, both called people to reform their lives and to a change of heart. And both stressed the urgency of this choice. Both were itinerant preachers rather than someone attached to the temple or a synagogue. And both of them gathered disciples.

But there were significant differences! John had the people come out to him in the desert. Jesus went to the people in their towns and villages and into their homes. John's message was a fiery one—threatening dire consequences to those who didn't take it to heart. The message of Jesus was a more joyful announcement of good news.

Jesus, unlike John, went out of his way to reach out to sinners—even to eat and drink with them. He also took the initiative to reach out to people who were poor and on the low end of society. The Gospels report no miracles by John, but the ministry of Jesus was filled with miracles, especially miracles of healing.

But perhaps the biggest difference of all is that although both John and Jesus preached repentance and reform, Jesus was more than a reformer. You might say that Jesus was a transformer. He changed the condition of the world by his entry into history and by sending his own Holy Spirit upon us. And John the Baptist recognized this difference himself! We hear him say in the Gospel today: "I baptize you with water for repentance, but one who is more powerful than I is coming after me. I am not worthy to carry his sandals. He will baptize you with the Holy Spirit and fire" (NRSV).

Advent is the beginning of a new Church year, and we're coming to the end of another calendar year. So, it's a natural time to think of changes we'd like to make in our lives.

What strikes me as I think about reform—and as I think about the difference between John and Jesus—is that we usually try to reform ourselves by using our own resources. It's sort of a self-help program! And in a way, John the Baptist preached that kind of reform. He spoke forcefully about the need for change, and then the people had to figure out how to do it. Jesus spoke differently. For example:

"Come to me, all you who labor and are burdened, and I will give you rest" (Matthew 11:28).

"I am the vine, you are the branches. Whoever remains in me and I in them will bear much fruit, because without me you can do nothing" (John 15:5).

The reform Jesus speaks about is never based on our own initiative or our own resources. We turn to him, not to our own self-help plan.

For starters, we need to turn to the Lord to find out what we should reform! Our own list can be a fairly stock one, and fairly superficial. We come up with things like: I've decided to lose some weight...or to stop smoking... Maybe we should do those things, but maybe that isn't where we should start!

Maybe we should start by turning to the Lord first, and asking: Lord, what is it that you want me to change in my life?

The Lord might say something like: Well, it would be good if you and I spent more time together. Or he might say: I'd like you to look at your relationships with other people—your family, or the people you work with, or a relationship that isn't so good. Or: The first thing I want you to do is reconcile with your sister whom you haven't spoken to in years.

I don't know what the Lord would say! But I do know we ought to give the Lord a chance to say it! Think of the difference it would make if I realized that something I need to change in my life isn't my idea! It's the Lord's idea. It's what the Lord is calling me to do. That's when I start taking it seriously! It's the Lord who's calling me to do this, or stop doing this. It might be the same thing I was thinking about, but now I realize that it comes from the Lord! It's a whole different story! And it's no longer a matter of doing it by the sheer force of my own will power. It's a matter of God's grace! And that's a major difference!

The source of true reform isn't our own initiative or our own resources. The source of true reform is the Lord who shapes us in his own image. Advent isn't a self-help program! It's a time when we try to open ourselves more fully to the Lord. The opening prayer of the Mass today is one we can take to heart because it speaks of the heart.

"God of power and mercy, open our hearts in welcome. Remove the things that hinder us from receiving Christ with joy, so that we may share his wisdom and become one with him."

That sounds like a pretty good plan!

THIRD SUNDAY OF ADVENT

First Reading: Isaiah 35:1–6, 10
Responsorial Psalm: 146
Second Reading: James 5:7–10
Gospel: Matthew 11:2–11

⚜

Last Sunday we heard from one of the principal players in the drama of Advent, John the Baptist. Again today, we meet him at a later point in his life. John is in prison now. And a lot has happened to him since we last heard him preaching and baptizing. You remember last week, John's message was: "Repent! For the Kingdom of Heaven is at hand!" (Matthew 3:2)

This was the fire that burned in his soul. He wasn't afraid to preach it to the religious establishment of his day. And he wasn't afraid to preach it to King Herod himself! And that's why he's in jail.

While he was in prison, John realized that his life would soon be over. And there was one thing he wanted to know before he died. So, in today's Gospel, John sends a message from prison to Jesus. "Are you the one who is to come, or should we look for another?" Was Jesus really the Messiah the Jewish world had been waiting for, or wasn't he? John needed to know.

Earlier on, when John had baptized Jesus in the desert, he had thought this surely is the one! But now, in prison, in the face of certain death, he has his doubts!

He has his doubts because things weren't working out the way he had expected. Jesus was not taking his advice. John had told the people that the ax was lying at the root ready to chop the unworthy trees down. John believed, as many of us do, that the best way to uproot evil is to do away with evil people! And here Jesus was—hanging out with the very people who were supposed to be chopped and burned, sitting down to dinner with people who deserved to be shunned. This wasn't in the script at all!

And the Baptist is feeling disappointed and disheartened. And sometimes that happens—particularly at Christmas. Christmas can be a uniquely painful season. It's the season to be merry. But it's not merry for everyone! For people who have lost a loved one in death, or people who have broken off a relationship with someone they've loved, this is the loneliest time of year. People who are sick, or discouraged, or alone find it extremely difficult to enter into the joy of this season.

A few years back, there was a haunting country song that had the words: "If we make it through December…" Some of you know the meaning of those words: "If we make it through December."

It was December for John the Baptist. He was hurting physically and emotionally. And he was disappointed because he had very different expectations of what the Messiah would be like. And of what the Messiah would do. And how he would go about doing it. John had been expecting the Messiah to come by storm! Where was the fiery avenger he had been foretelling?

Sometimes we're disappointed, not because what we receive is bad, but because what we receive is not what we expected! Our expectations were flawed.

There may be people here this morning who feel that life has somehow cheated them. But I'd wager that if you lost everything you have right now, and then suddenly had it all restored, you'd feel very grateful indeed! The problem is not what we have. The problem is what we expect to have! And we become so invested in our own expectations! And when they're not met, we can begin to doubt the very existence of God.

Jesus was a scandal for most of his contemporaries. He upset their expectations! They believed he was going to act according to their plans. They believed the Messiah would reveal a God who rewarded the just and punished sinners. What Jesus revealed was a God whose solution to the problem of evil is to overcome the evil— not by violence, but by goodness and gentleness!

The crowd that cheered him as he rode into Jerusalem on a donkey that Palm Sunday morning believed he was going to a coronation. And, of course, he was going to a crucifixion! Who would not find that Messiah shocking, and a profound disappointment?

Who would ever expect to find God on a cross? And who expects to be asked to carry a cross? Have you noticed that the cross that comes to us is never a good one? It's always the wrong one! We would so much rather have another cross—one according to our taste, and made to our measurements.

So, the Baptist, languishing in prison over a Messiah he didn't quite understand, is someone we can identify with. We have our own John the Baptist moments. They come when we're in the prison of our own struggles of discouragement and desolation. But like John, we have to hang on—in trust and love, and be reminded that God's ways are not our ways. We often hope God will work a miracle and transform the unhappy circumstances in our lives. Instead, God does something better! God comes to share them!

"Here I am," God says, "let me be with you." "Let me be with you in your disappointments. Let me help you rise above your disappointments. And above your expectations. Let me be with you in whatever life deals you." This is the God whom John struggled to know and whose birth we will celebrate just two weeks from today.

FOURTH SUNDAY
OF ADVENT

First Reading: Isaiah 7:10–14
Responsorial Psalm: 24
Second Reading: Romans 1:1–7
Gospel: Matthew 1:18–24

For the first time in the Sundays of Advent, we hear the improbable story of the birth of Jesus this morning! In Matthew's telling of it, Joseph has the critical role. The fulfillment of Old Testament prophecy will depend on him. Because Joseph is a descendant of King David, any child of his will have the bloodline of the promised Messiah. Matthew is writing for Jewish Christians, so it's very important for him to link Jesus to David's bloodline. All the Jewish prophets had foretold the Messiah would be in the line of David.

So, the critical event for Matthew in this story this morning is the annunciation to Joseph. You notice there's no Mary in the picture at all! Mary has no words to speak. Joseph is the important one. Because for Matthew, the whole grand experiment hangs on what happens to him. If Joseph believes the angel, everything is on! The story can continue. And her child will be born "The Son of David." But if Joseph does not believe, then everything grinds to a halt!

The child to be born is Joseph's until he says otherwise. Because the issue at stake, the paternity issue, is not a biological one in this Jewish culture, but a legal one. If a man were to claim: "This is my child," then the law would certify that and protect that. So, will Joseph claim the child, or won't he? Will he believe the impossible? Or will he stick with what makes sense to him and send Mary away to bear the child in disgrace?

According to Matthew, Joseph's belief is as crucial to the story as Mary's womb! It takes both parents to give birth to this remarkable child. Mary to give him life, and Joseph to give him a lineage— "Jesus, son of David."

So, Joseph is at the heart of this Gospel story this morning. He wakes up one day to find his life wrecked. His fiancé pregnant, his trust betrayed. He wakes up one morning to find a mess he had nothing to do with. And he decides to believe that God is present in it!

Joseph claims the scandal! And he gives it his name. He legitimizes it. And "the mess" becomes the place where the Messiah is born!

So, Joseph is the one to watch in this story today. He's the one who is most like us! Because every day we face circumstances beyond our control. And we're tempted to divorce ourselves from it all. And then a voice whispers in our ear: "Do not fear. God is here. It may not be the life you had planned, but God can be born here too...if you will allow that!"

The real shocker is that God's "yes" depends on our own "yes." That God's birth requires human partners! A Mary. A Joseph. Willing to believe the impossible! Willing to claim the scandal, to adopt it.

Matthew writes: "When Joseph awoke, he did as the angel had commanded him and took his wife into his home." Joseph believed! And so, the whole impossible scenario was able to proceed!

My prayer this morning, as we draw near to Christmas, is that we may believe that God is with us. With us in our life right now, such as it is, with its ups and downs, its joys and sorrows, its hopes and anxieties. It's into that mix that God was born, and in that mix that God can still be found.

SEASON OF
CHRISTMAS

CHRISTMAS
(MASS DURING THE DAY)

First Reading: Isaiah 52:7–10
Responsorial Psalm: 98
Second Reading: Hebrews 1:1–6
Gospel: John 1:1–18 or 1:1–5, 9–14

It's difficult to live with the prolonged silence of those we love! It's even MORE difficult to live with the silence of the God who loves us!

It's a truth of ancient religion that the wisdom of God was hidden and wrapped in silence. That silence was hard to bear! The psalmist in the twenty-second psalm wrote in desperation: "O my God. I call by day, and you give no reply. I call by night, and I find no peace."

But God *did* speak! As our second reading today (from the Letter to the Hebrews) tells us: "In times past, God spoke in partial and various ways to our ancestors through the prophets." God spoke *through* the silence…and called on the people to stay faithful to their commitment to Him.

But who could have guessed that one day, God would speak a word like Jesus?

At the heart of our Christian faith, is the belief that the most precious word God spoke became a *person*!

The same Letter to the Hebrews today goes on to say that God "has spoken to us through the Son."

The word of God became flesh in Jesus! The great silence of God was broken forever!

At Christmas, we celebrate the great truth that God is not wrapped in silence but wrapped in the swaddling clothes of an infant and laid in a manger. He is the one who will show us how *close* God is! Who will teach us to call God *Father*. And will die to prove the measure of God's love for us.

For us, and for millions of people since the birth of Christ, we have a new way not just of understanding life, but a new way of living it! For 20 centuries, untold numbers of people have been grasped by this child from Bethlehem, have been caught up in his message, and who have had their lives profoundly changed by him!

We are numbered among them today.

Let us rejoice in the One who reveals the face of God to us! And who is forever God *with us*!

May you have a blessed Christmas!

HOLY FAMILY

First Reading: Sirach 3:2–6, 12–14
Responsorial Psalm: 128:1–5
Second Reading: Colossians 3:12–21 or 3:12–17
Gospel: Matthew 2:13–15, 19–23

❧

Christmas is not over! The Church continues to celebrate Christmas this Sunday, and again next Sunday—the Feast of the Epiphany—and all through the week after Epiphany. Christmas is just too big a celebration to be over with in a single day!

And, of course, Christmas is a very family-oriented time of year. Last Sunday, I met a number of parishioners who wished me a Happy Christmas that day because they weren't going to be here on Christmas Day. They were going home for Christmas to be with their families.

So, given that Christmas is such a family-oriented time, it's not surprising that the Church designates this Sunday as the Feast of the Holy Family of Jesus, Mary and Joseph. The feast doesn't have a long history. It began at the end of the First World War as a way of trying to strengthen family life that had suffered so much from the war. Of course, family life has changed a lot since the First World War. And it continues to change.

We know that an increasing number of marriages are ending in divorce, and people who remarry often bring children from earlier marriages, and this leads to what is being called: blended families. There's a big discussion these days about what constitutes a family. The traditional view that a family is made up of a stay-at-home mother, a working father, and their biological children is too restrictive. You know that there's an increasing number of two career families today—mother and father both working full-time. There are single parent families and same-sex couples with adopted children. Some couples have no children at all due to infertility problems, while other couples choose not to have children. So, a family takes on many shapes these days.

But I think what's more important than the question of: "What constitutes a family?" is the question: "How does a family function together?" If people share life together, respect each other, care for each other, and enable each other to thrive and flourish, then they're a healthy family. If there's verbal or emotional abuse, betrayal of trust, or mistreatment, this is going to produce a dysfunctional family. Quality of life should be the key issue in any discussion of family.

In 1988, the American bishops wrote a letter to Catholics in the country on the topic of family life. There's just one sentence in that letter I want to cite. The bishops wrote: "The family has a special vocation to be a place where people are loved, not for what they have, or for what they do, but simply because they are."

I think this is so true, and so important! People are desperate to know this kind of love, and home should be the place where they learn it. The family should be the one place where people can feel free to be themselves. Where they can find love and acceptance, forgiveness and encouragement. I'm reminded of the saying of Robert Frost where he describes the family home as the place where, when you have to go there, they have to take you in" (Frost, "The Death of the Hired Man"). Somewhere along the line, a child has to hear the message: You are loved for who you are, and you have a right to be who you are. You have a right to be yourself and to possess your own feelings in your own way, but in a way that's respectful of others.

The family is where we learn from one another, and where

we're strengthened by one another. Jesus learned what love is from his parents. He learned to love at home! That's why this feast today is so practical. It goes to the heart of everyday life. Most all of us lead good Christian lives not by doing things that are heroic or unusual, but simply by being a loving parent, a loving spouse, a loving son or daughter, a loving sibling. And this is learned in the home. Or it becomes terribly difficult ever to learn at all.

All the social commentators say that the well-being of society is dependent on the healthy state of family life, however you understand the term "family." I've heard one social commentator, Joseph Califano from the National Center on Addiction and Substance Abuse at Columbia University, identify four family qualities that greatly reduce the probability that a child will grow up to abuse alcohol or drugs:

1st)   The family regularly shares meals together,
2nd) The parents help children with homework,
3rd)   The parents impose a curfew on their children, and
4th)   The family observes some form of religious practice in the home.

Studies show that children from such families have the best chance of escaping the scourge of alcohol and drug abuse. These four family qualities sound so simple, but I wonder how often all four of them are found in the same family!

I'm reminded today, Holy Family Sunday, of a story told by Fr. Lawrence Jenco. You may remember that name. Fr. Jenco was the priest abducted in Lebanon in 1985 and held prisoner for a year and a half, along with some other Americans. He told a story a few years ago about visiting his mother in the hospital as she lay dying.

As he approached her hospital bed, she tried to speak to him, but he couldn't hear her. Her voice was too weak. So, he bent close to hear her last words of wisdom—words that would surely be filled with great meaning and insight. With great effort, she clearly whispered: "Did you have lunch?" She died within the hour.

I thought of this today because I think this is a Holy Family story. I think Fr. Jenco learned how to relate to other people, and how to forgive those who had imprisoned him, because he had learned love and forgiveness at home. Because his mother had modeled that for him. Because his mother on her death bed was thinking of the well-being of others. Even in the hour of her death, her thoughts and concern were turned toward others.

And I think of the story of a mother of ten children who once said: "The one I love the most is the one that's sick until she's well, and the one away from home until he comes back!"

May the members of your family discover what love really is in the new year!

SOLEMNITY OF MARY, MOTHER OF GOD

First Reading: Numbers 6:22–27
Responsorial Psalm: 67
Second Reading: Galatians 4:4–7
Gospel: Luke 2:16–21

❧

Tonight's feast has had many themes over the years. It's the Feast of Mary, the Mother of God. That's a title that was fought over in the early centuries of the Church. Mary was the mother of Jesus of Nazareth. The question was: Can she be called "the Mother of God!"? The third ecumenical council of the Church in the year 431 decided that she could, and the feast of Mary under that title has been celebrated ever since.

Tonight's feast is also the Octave of Christmas, and the Church celebrates Christmas all over again tonight. The liturgy is still pondering the birth of Jesus. And so, we have this Gospel from Luke—the visit of the shepherds to Mary and Joseph and the newborn Jesus. I think the key verse here in this Gospel is this one: "Mary kept all these things, reflecting on them in her heart." We're not told what the shepherds said to her, but whatever it was, it had a tremendous importance for her. And she continued to reflect on it in her heart—which is another way of saying she prayed about it! And I imagine she prayed about it often throughout her lifetime.

While events surrounding the birth of Jesus are very much on my mind tonight, so is this special night itself. Tonight is also New Year's Eve! I confess to being somewhat of a sentimentalist about New Year's Eve. And for many people, it's a time for making New Year's resolutions.

On this special night, I'd like to suggest something else. I suggest you spend some quiet time looking back over the past year and thanking God for the year. This is not always an easy thing to do. It may have been a year of struggle for you, of poor health, of sorrows, of friends and relatives lost to death. A year of one disappointment, or of one hurt, after another.

The world itself has had a hard year: there's been the rise of more terrorism and the unspeakable tragedy it's causing throughout the Middle East. Our military is still too involved in many dangerous parts of the world. And our Congress has hit an historic low in its inability to work together for the good of the nation. How do we thank God for the past year when this is how it's been?

For Christians, when all is said and done, I think we have to believe that God is still running the world! And that despite the tragedies and the sorrows, God is somewhere to be found in everything that happens to us.

Giving thanks to God for every circumstance in life is not a new idea! Three thousand years ago, the ancient Jews formulated *blessings—berakhot* in Hebrew—blessings for the bad as well as for the good in life—because all life, they believed, comes from God. We Christians believe that too!

Whenever we gather here for the Eucharist, what we're thanking God for is the whole of Christ's life—his birth as well as his violent death. We don't bless just the good parts of his life here, and curse the rest. Because we believe that it's all a single tapestry, that it all fits together and that you can't remove a single thread!

I think the challenge, as we look back over the past year, is to see our own lives in the same way! To learn how to give thanks at this altar not only for the mixed blessings of Christ's life but also for the mixed blessings of our own! To say "Thank You" for the whole mixed bag! For the things we welcome, as well as the things we would want to avoid.

The image that comes to mind is the way we read Scripture here at Mass. When the lector finishes the reading, the lector pauses for a moment to let it sink in and then says: "The Word of the Lord."

Then it's the congregation's turn to *accept* that word by responding: "Thanks be to God." That's an easy thing to say when the reading has been comforting and has been about God's goodness to us.

But what about those readings that seem full of doom and judgment? The lector announces: "The Word of the Lord!" And we know what our response is to be! "Thanks be to God," we say! Because we believe God is somewhere to be found in everything that happens to us.

"Thanks be to God," we say, because we believe that God's love and grace is always there, however dark or painful our path through life may sometimes be.

God is God, and our lives are our lives, and we can love them or curse them, give thanks for them or waste them away with regret. I suggest tonight that you look back over your life in the past year, and accept it, embrace it. And know that every single happening was meant as an invitation to you to draw closer to God, and to experience God's presence in your life. And know that every single happening has that potential!

So, as we come to the end of the year, I wish you a Happy New Year! Whether you leave here tonight to join friends and family, or whether you're alone for the evening—whether you stay awake to usher in the New Year, or whether you hope to be asleep by then— know that God goes with you tonight as you leave our church, and that there's no corner of your life that God does not inhabit!

So, keep watch for God in the New Year! God is there! And let our response be: Thanks be to God!

EPIPHANY

First Reading: Isaiah 60:1–6
Responsorial Psalm: 72
Second Reading: Ephesians 3:2–3a, 5–6
Gospel: Matthew 2:1–12

❧

Two weeks ago, we were celebrating Christmas! And today's feast is a kind of second celebration of Christmas. The Epiphany is what someone once called "Christmas all over again without the bother." In some countries of the world, this day is more important than Christmas Day itself! And it's the day on which gifts are exchanged.

This Gospel story today has been a favorite of Christians for centuries! We love to hear it. It gives us some of the richest imagery in the Church's liturgical year: three wise men traveling on their camels in the night, across the desert, guided by one large, bright star.

We like to see them appear at our creches with their royal clothes and their precious gifts. What did Matthew have in mind when he told this exotic story?

Well, I think Matthew wanted to tell us something very fundamental to the Christian gospel. Matthew sees the three visitors to the crib as representing all non-Jewish people, all the other nations and cultures—foreigners who are open to receiving this child and who want to worship him. And so, the opening prayer of the Mass today reads: "You revealed your Son to the nations by the guidance of a star." And in the first reading from Isaiah, we heard this: "Nations shall walk by your light," and "the wealth of Nations shall be brought to you."

Paul, in the second reading from Ephesians, writes that the mystery hidden from former generations has now been revealed, namely, that the Gentiles are "coheirs" with Jews. They are members of the same body and co-partners in the promise of Christ Jesus. Or as another translation puts it: "I reveal to you a mystery which God revealed to me: namely, God's secret plan to include the Gentiles in God's kindness" (alt. translation).

What the Feast of Epiphany is saying is that Christ has come for everyone! This is the larger meaning of Christmas—in case we missed it! And it's today's Feast of the Epiphany that reveals it. "Come to me, everyone. I'm here for everyone. No one is excluded." That's the really good news for Christmas!

Up until the Epiphany, everything in the Christmas drama has been overwhelmingly Jewish! Advent was about the Jewish expectation for the Messiah. And all the main characters of the Christmas drama are Jewish, of course. So up until now, something has been missing!

And what's been missing is the non-Jewish world!

The last act comes today with the arrival of the three wise men from the East. The Epiphany star invites the Jews to move over— and to make room for the Gentiles! All God's children are to be included!

What disturbing news that must have been for the Jewish people of the first century! To be told to move over and make room for the Gentiles, who are now included in the kindness of God! Exclusion was part of their Jewish religion. It was built into their very temple where they had constructed a stone wall to divide the outer court of the Gentiles from the inner court of the Jews. That wall separated the chosen Jew from the unchosen Gentile!

St. Paul, writing to the Christian converts in Ephesus in the letter we hear this morning, reminds them: "Christ has made peace between Jews and Gentiles by making us all one family, by breaking down the wall of contempt that used to separate us" (Ephesians 2:14, alt. translation).

Christ was about tearing walls *down*, and building *bridges* between people! That's so very clear as you read through the Gospels!

We know that popes are frequently identified as *pontiffs*, and that the word literally means bridge builder! Pope Francis—since the beginning of his papacy—has been reaching out to Catholics who have felt excluded from the Church because of their marital status, or their sexuality—despite what their consciences tell them. And some Catholics, unfortunately, have been critical of the pope for doing that!

Fundamentalist religion is bent on scattering God's children and creating infidels that it can exclude from God's care and goodness. And to the extent religion excludes *any* of God's children from the kindness of God, it's *false*! To the extent it gathers and *includes*, it's true!

All the great religious stories need a star of the Epiphany to purify them of their dark side—a dark side that seeks to *exclude* rather than *include* others.

That inclusion is what we pray for on this Feast of the Epiphany.

BAPTISM OF THE LORD

First Reading: Isaiah 42:1–4, 6–7
Responsorial Psalm: 29
Second Reading: Acts 10:34–38
Gospel: Matthew 3:13–17

Every year we leap from yesterday's Feast of the Epiphany to this Feast of the Baptism of the Lord. Every year, the liturgical calendar jumps thirty years of Christ's life in under one week's time!

That leap in years is prompted by the Gospels themselves. The Gospels seem to imply, in those thirty years, that nothing of great importance happened. A very ordinary life. That is, until today!

Today changes everything. The baptism was the turning point in Jesus' life. After this, he no longer goes back to being the carpenter in Nazareth. He leaves behind the hidden, private life he had in a small town and launches out into the much broader world of the whole of Palestine.

Why did he ever want to undergo this Jewish religious ceremony? As water was being poured over their heads, people confessed their sins and repented! Why did Jesus get himself involved in that kind of scene? Surely not because he had sins to be sorry about.

He went to John for baptism because he wanted to, not because he needed to. He wanted to do what everyone else was doing! He wanted to identify as closely as possible with the sinful men and women he lived among.

So, he takes the plunge! He gets wet with all those who are standing in the muddy waters of humanity. And, to one degree or another, that's all of us.

How wonderful of him to stand with them all in the mud and allow the river water to flow over his head in a gesture of cleansing.

If there is just one scene in the life of Jesus that should convince us of his solidarity with us and his sympathy for sinners, it's this one of his baptism.

Here Jesus stands with all men and women of every age, and of every generation—in a gesture that cries out: I am with you! I am with you in your humanity!

SEASON OF LENT

ASH WEDNESDAY

First Reading: Joel 2:12–18 or Isaiah 58:1–12
Responsorial Psalm: 51
Second Reading: 2 Corinthians 5:20—6:2
Gospel: Matthew 6:1–6, 16–18

We begin Lent today with ashes. And ashes are a great symbol. They have a way of putting things in proper perspective. When we receive ashes, we're being reminded of our own mortality, our own corruptibility. Because everything turns to ashes! Everything! This material world, all our prized possessions, our homes, the clothes we're wearing, our bodies, the bodies of those we love—they all turn to ashes. Because God has something better in mind, something greater in store for us. And we need to be connected to that greater thing. We need to be growing spiritually.

There are two sets of words that can be used when ashes are placed on your forehead in the form of a cross. One set of words is this: "Remember that you are dust and to dust you will return." What a very sobering thought that is, but very true! And every once in a while, it's very good to be reminded of that truth!

A newer, alternate formula for the imposition of ashes is this: "Turn away from sin and be faithful to the Gospel." These words are more in keeping with the prayers and readings of the Masses during Lent. Lent is turning time, or conversion time! The word *conversion* means literally to turn around, to change direction. For

Christians, conversion really means to change the direction in which we're looking for happiness! Sometimes that change will be dramatic, maybe even 180 degrees! But for most of us it's not that sensational. It may be more like a 20-degree turn, but it's a turn that should make a real difference.

"Return to me with your whole heart," were the first words we heard in the Scripture readings this morning. And as Lent goes on, we'll notice how frequently that word "turn," or "turning," comes up in the prayers and readings of the Mass. Here are two typical prayers from Masses in the first week of Lent.

"Lord, be close to your people and let us turn to you with all our hearts."

And this one:

"I do not wish the sinner to die, says the Lord, but to turn to me and live."

Today is a good time to ask myself: "In what direction have I been looking for happiness? Might God be calling me to turn a little more in the right direction? A different direction?"

Turn to God and live! That's the message of the Bible in a nutshell. And it's what Lent is focused on. Lent is not so much a time to remind us that we're burdened with sins. Rather, it's a time to turn to the One who takes away our burdens!

So, what turning movements are you going to make this Lent? This really deserves your serious thinking. It's not enough just to come up for ashes. That's very superficial. And it's much too easy. Nothing's going to change in your life by having ashes rubbed on your forehead! In a few moments, I, and the ministers of the Eucharist, will come forward and distribute ashes. But don't come up unless you really want to do something serious for Lent, unless you want to turn to the Lord, and live!

We ask you to come up on a double line in the middle aisle, and return by the side aisles. We don't give ashes to children for the simple reason that children are not capable of sin. We give ashes only to sinners. Children may come forward for a blessing, but let the sinners come forward now, please!

First Sunday of Lent

First Reading: Genesis 2:7–9; 3:1–7
Responsorial Psalm: 51:3–6, 12–13, 17
Second Reading: Romans 5:12–19 or 5:12, 17–19
Gospel: Matthew 4:1–11

The Gospel we hear on this first Sunday of Lent is always one of the accounts of our Lord's struggle with temptation at the end of his forty-day fast in the desert. Always, at the beginning of Lent, we see Jesus in a situation not unlike some of the situations we face. We often struggle with temptation in our own life. We speak of "temptations"—in the plural, but really, they all come down to one basic temptation. We want to be like God. Being human has too many limitations for us.

Look at the story of Adam and Eve we hear today. All those trees in the garden are theirs for the asking, except one. And they couldn't avoid that one tree! They couldn't accept any limitation. And that's the fundamental limitation we all face. We don't say "I want to be like God." But what we want is to get around some of the things involved in being human.

The core of being human is sometimes having to "die," figuratively or literally. We have to "die" in order to get to life. And we have a resistance to that from the very beginning. When we were in our mother's womb, we didn't want to be born. We didn't want to die to the world of her womb, and be born into this world.

Now it's interesting to think about this from the other side. What do you think it's like to be like God?

To be God is to be all-powerful. And you can use that power to get anything you want.

But the God revealed to us in Scripture is not that kind of God! The image of God that comes through in Scripture speaks of a God who is like a father or mother—who sometimes worries about the children. A God who loves them, and is sometimes hurt by their failure to love in return. A God who sometimes gets angry with them. We don't really know what it's like to be God.

What we know is that God became one of us—and fully accepted his humanity. This means that often we have to die to the self, to the ego, in order to live.

We can be sure of that, because what's the first thing that happens to him when he begins his ministry? The devil comes and tests him, to see if he can avoid his human limitations. The devil says, in effect: You don't have to go through all this human stuff. You are the Son of God! So, change these stones to bread. If you're hungry, eat. If you feel like it, fling yourself off the temple. You can do anything you want. You can take over all the kingdoms of the world!

Jesus rejected the temptation. He stood strong as a full-fledged human being. He accepted the limitations of space and time and power. And because he was truly human, one of us, he sometimes felt frustration.

When he came down from the mountain of the Transfiguration, he found the rest of the disciples arguing with a crowd about a cure. And he says to them: "How much longer must I be with you? How much longer must I put up with you?" (Matthew 17:17, NRSV). And, when his disciples are concerned about not having bread, even after Jesus fed the crowds of thousands with a few loaves, he asks them: "Do you not yet understand? Do you have eyes and not see, ears and not hear?" (Mark 8:17–18)

Of course, the biggest struggle Jesus had was facing death! In Gethsemane he bares his soul to God. He prays: "Father, all things are possible to you. Take this cup away from me" (Mark 14:36).

Now that prayer has an echo, doesn't it, of essentially what the devil said in the desert: "If you are the Son of God, you can do anything you want. All things are possible to you." But Jesus adds to his own prayer these words: "Not what I will, Father, but what you will" (Mark 14:36). And in praying that way, he fully accepts what it is to be a human being.

So, I think our Scripture this morning is sending two important messages for Lent.

First: Accept what it is to be a human being. Accept the limitations of your humanity. And know that your humanity is a great gift from God.

And secondly: Realize that dying, whether figuratively—in the many small ways we die to self—or literally—when we take our last breath—those dyings are the only way to fullness of life.

SECOND SUNDAY OF LENT

First Reading: Genesis 12:1–4a
Responsorial Psalm: 33
Second Reading: 2 Timothy 1:8b–10
Gospel: Matthew 17:1–9

I think both major readings today—this Gospel and the first reading from Genesis about Abraham—are stories about trust in God. How do we learn to trust?

I remember some years ago, when I was living at our retreat house on Staten Island, we would occasionally have day programs for eighth-graders preparing for Confirmation.

One of the things we often did was to send the children out on what was called "a trust walk." We would gather a group of about thirty youngsters, blindfold half of them, and then send them out in pairs—one child blindfolded, the other not. And they were asked to explore the property.

It was quite a sight to see! Over a dozen blindfolded children walking around with someone at their side to hold onto. It was a wonderful way to learn trust! It was a wonderful way to learn what it feels like to be totally dependent on someone else to guide you, so you won't stumble and fall.

I think something like this is going on in the two main Scripture stories today. God is teaching people to trust him.

That first reading from the twelfth chapter of Genesis gives us just a tiny part of the story of Abraham. The history of the Jewish nation begins with this man. It begins with God's call to Abraham to set out from where he was living—in modern day Iraq—and to go where God would lead him, to the land that is modern Israel.

God makes a startling promise to Abraham. This man—who was already seventy-five years old and whose wife had been barren—will become the father of a great nation!

Abraham sets out from home, not knowing the route he was going to take, and not knowing where the journey would end. He sets out with only the promise from God that God was going to lead him. The question of how is not spelled out for him in advance. It would be worked out on the way!

Now I think this is what Jesus is trying to teach Peter, James, and John in the Gospel today when he takes them with him to the mountain top. By letting them see the dramatic change that came over him, Jesus was inviting them to a very deep level of trust as they faced a very uncertain future.

All the Gospel writers tell us that this dramatic scene on the mountain top took place just after Jesus had finished telling the Twelve that we would have to suffer much and be put to death. They didn't want to hear that, of course, and they were going to be shattered by it when it happened...particularly Peter, James, and John—the three he takes with him to the mountain top. These are the same three who will be with him in the garden of Gethsemane the night before his death. There they will see him at his lowest. So today, on the mountain top, he lets them see his glory—as a kind of counterbalance and a strength to hold onto in the future.

And notice how Peter reacts. He is so overcome by the vision of Christ in glory that he wants to build tents and stay all night. It was a typically human reaction. And it happens to us all the time.

We look at the crest of the wave we're riding, and we say: "Let's freeze the moment! Let's keep it like this forever." We want the moments of deep joy to continue.

But of course, realism comes along and says that's impossible. We have to come down from the mountain top and return to ordinary, everyday life—and to life's disappointments and absurdities. For the life of faith is not life on the mountain top! The mountain top experiences help to build trust in God, but trust is lived out on the level stretches of ground—at the foot of the mountain.

And to live and walk there is often to walk in the dark as those blindfolded school children at the retreat house had to do. You learn to walk in darkness. But you're not walking alone.

You're never alone!

THIRD SUNDAY OF LENT

First Reading: Exodus 17:3–7
Responsorial Psalm: 95
Second Reading: Romans 5:1–2, 5–8
Gospel: John 4:5–42 or 4:5–15, 19b–26, 39a, 40–42

❧

This Gospel story I've just read is heard once every three years, on this third Sunday in Lent. What I like so much about the story is that it's a very personal encounter between Jesus and the woman. It's just the two of them together. They must have talked for a long while. How else could Jesus have known about her tangled life? And how else could she have opened her heart to him?

I sometimes like to imagine myself meeting Jesus in a similar way—he and I sitting down together and talking about things that matter most to him and to me. What would I have to tell him? What would he say to me? What would he reveal to me about himself? And what would he tell me about myself?

I don't think this scenario is just pure daydreaming! I believe that scene is part of my future. I believe I'm going to meet Jesus face-to-face one day. Don't you? Isn't this part of what life after death means to you?

St. Paul, in his First Letter to the Corinthians, says we know God in this life only in a very partial and imperfect way. But after death, I will know God as completely as God knows me! He writes:

"Now we see only a dim reflection in a mirror. But then we shall see God face to face!" (1 Corinthians 13:12, NRSV).

This Gospel scene today is a kind of preview of that. It shows a very human Jesus, tired and thirsty after walking in the heat of the noonday sun. He sits down to rest at a well, hoping someone would come along with one of those leather pouches that acted as a bucket for retrieving well water. Someone does come along, and before long some wonderful mutual disclosure is going on.

It's hard for us to imagine how very unusual this whole scene was. Most Jews wouldn't have entered Samaritan territory at all! They would have detoured around it. When the Samaritan woman came along, Jesus strikes up a conversation with her!

We learn that the woman is something of a social outcast. She's had five husbands and is now living with a sixth man. The Gospel writer is careful to note the hour. She's coming at a time when she knows she can avoid meeting other women who come in the early morning. They undoubtedly dislike her and shun her. But Jesus gets into a long conversation with her! And he winds up disclosing who he is to her!

This is really quite amazing! Of all places for him to find an open, hungry heart—in Samaria—the one place Jews avoided! And of all the Samaritans to have a curiosity for what he was about: a woman with a very checkered past! She becomes the first person in the Gospels to whom Jesus openly and without ambiguity reveals himself as Messiah! How remarkable!

The story also reveals Jesus as the long-awaited Savior of his people. It tells us about the gift he has to offer—what he calls "living water." "Living water" was the common expression for a flowing water source, like a spring or a gushing fountain. Such streams are rare in the Middle East, so people depended on rainwater that was collected in local wells. When Jesus offers to give the woman water that will keep on flowing, of course she's delighted, but confused. She doesn't understand that the water he's speaking of is actually a new life—the life of Jesus—that will come inside her and flow within her.

The early Christians saw in these words of Jesus a beautiful description of what happens at Baptism! The offer Jesus is making to the woman, and the offer he makes to anyone being baptized, is this: "Let me live in you. Let me make my home in you."

The ways of God are quite wonderful, aren't they? God takes the first step, God reaches out to us, not because of who we are, but because of who God is!

This is what St. Paul is speaking about in that second reading today. Paul is amazed that while we were still sinners, Jesus died for us! Jesus doesn't wait for us to turn away from sin, as much as he wants that to happen. Even while I'm doing the wrong thing, God comes to me and thirsts for me! Isn't that amazing? God offers the gift of living water, that is to say, God offers the gift of God's own life—to people who are dead, or as good as dead—even when the gift is not sought after and not deserved!

The woman in the story has no special claim to the living water Jesus offers her. But no matter. He's totally accepting of her for who she is. An unworthy person, with no claim on God, is offered a new lease on life!

And so, we pray this morning: God of compassion and God of second chances, satisfy our thirst. Give us a fuller share in your own divine life. Come and live in us.

Fourth Sunday of Lent

First Reading: 1 Samuel 16:1b, 6–7, 10–13a
Responsorial Psalm: 23
Second Reading: Ephesians 5:8–14
Gospel: John 9:1–41 or 9:1, 6–9, 13–17, 34–38

❧

Last Sunday the Gospel gave us the dramatic story of the Lord's meeting with the Samaritan woman at the well. As you may remember, a good deal of conversation and interaction went on between them in that story, and the woman walked away a changed person.

Well, today we have another long and dramatic Gospel, and there are so many things that might be said about it. There's the question the disciples put to Jesus about innocent human suffering and its connection with sin. This is a question that has troubled people since the beginning of time.

The common understanding among Jews in the time of Jesus was that sickness was a result of sin. In our own time we have sometimes heard this—in discussions about AIDS, for example. That AIDS is God's punishment for sinful behavior.

Jesus assures his disciples that this man's blindness was not a punishment for his sin, or for any sins of his parents. And this answer he gave is pure gold as we try to grapple with the mystery of human suffering! Blindness or any other affliction or disease is not a punishment from God.

Fourth Sunday of Lent

I want to say something today about the cure in this Gospel story. On one level, it's a cure from physical blindness. The cure happens not instantaneously, but over a period of time. We don't know how long a time. First, Jesus had to make a kind of paste out of mud and saliva. Then he smeared the man's eyes with the paste, and then the man went off to a place called the Pool of Siloam and he washed his eyes in the waters. Only after that was he cured. This process corresponds more closely with the way illness is normally cured today through the miracles of modern medicine. A person's cancer, for instance, is declared cured—but only after months, maybe years, of treatment. Instantaneous cures are few and far between.

On a deeper level, another cure goes on in the blind man. Something even more wonderful than the gift of sight is given to him. He comes to different degrees of faith in Jesus. You notice that at first, he knows Jesus simply as "that man they call Jesus." Later, when the Pharisees question him, Jesus is something more for him. Now he calls him "a prophet" and "this man from God." Finally, when Jesus himself seeks him out, the man born blind addresses him as "Lord" and falls down and worships him! So, there's a progressing coming to faith here that corresponds to our own experience of faith, doesn't it? In our own lives, faith grows slowly and in stages—sometimes in fits and starts—and only over a considerable period of time and challenge. That wonderful opening verse we heard in the second reading from Paul to the Ephesians easily applies to the blind man of this Gospel story. We hear Paul say: "There was a time when you were darkness, but now you are light in the Lord." That gift, the gift of insight into who Jesus is, is a greater gift than the gift of physical sight!

It would have been wonderful if the Pharisees had been open to receiving this gift of insight as well. They prided themselves on their knowledge of the ways of God. But Jesus did not adhere to the rule. The rule said: no healings on the Sabbath. Only if there was a life-threatening situation were you permitted to intervene, and that was to keep the situation from getting worse—not to make it better!

Break your leg, and it had to remain unset. The blind man was not in a life-threatening situation. So, by bringing healing to him on the Sabbath, Jesus was breaking the third great commandment: "Keep holy the Sabbath Day." If Jesus wanted to heal him, he should have waited another day.

The Pharisees jump on him for this! They don't approve of what he's done. It doesn't fit their understanding of the commandments, and so they condemn him. And here is the irony of the story. The main character in this story is blind, yet the Pharisees are really the blind ones! They think they see, don't realize they're blind, and prefer to remain blind and in the dark rather than to come into the light Jesus is offering them.

So, I say, beware of people who think they have all the answers. Even within Catholicism. God is too big ever to be captured and forced into a neat box. I think one of the great lessons of this Gospel today might be put this way: Even though you know all there's to know about Scripture, and even though you know the history of the Church and its traditions inside out, be prepared for some surprises! Because God is full of surprises!

FIFTH SUNDAY OF LENT

First Reading: Ezekiel 37:12–14
Responsorial Psalm: 130
Second Reading: Romans 8:8–11
Gospel: John 11:1–45 or 11:3–7, 17, 20–27, 33b–45

I think it's fair to say that when God speaks to us through the Sacred Scriptures, God's word is always about life and the things that lead to life, not to death. This is especially true in these Scripture readings today. Lazarus comes out of his tomb today, and the Jewish people in exile go home.

It can feel very much like death to be exiled. We're seeing unprecedented instances of this in our own time. A report from the United Nations a year ago disclosed that the number of people displaced from their homes due to conflict and persecution exceeded 60 million for the first time in the United Nation's history!

Many of these exiles are in a situation not too unlike the situation described in our first reading today. About six hundred years before Christ, the Jewish people were driven into exile to a place very near the modern city of Baghdad. Here they were homeless for about fifty years. The prophet Ezekiel, writing from this exile, has a vision of a field of dried-up bones. This is what exile felt like to him. It's the way dead bones in a graveyard would feel if they could feel anything at all.

Ezekiel dreams of a time when Israel would be restored to its own land—when God would breathe life into those dry, dead bones. He was convinced this would happen, though God alone knew when. But Ezekiel lived in that hope. And, of course, it did happen. Historians tell us the Jewish exiles began to go home in 538 BC, and they began to rebuild Jerusalem.

Something even more wonderful happens in this Gospel story this morning. This is a story, not about the evils of exile. It's a story about the ultimate evil of death itself.

The sisters of Lazarus, Martha and Mary, were deeply grieved by his death. And they felt Jesus could have prevented it. They had sent word to him. They thought he would come at once. But instead, Jesus stayed where he was for two more days! He could have been there in a matter of hours. Why did he wait? How would you feel if a loved one took ill, and you sent for your close friend, the doctor, and the doctor waited forty-eight hours before answering you?

When Jesus finally does arrive, he finds that Lazarus has been dead for four days! His sisters are distraught. What can be more hopeless than being dead for four whole days! Jesus himself is deeply grieved. He breaks down and weeps openly. Death has a sting even the Lord of life fully experiences! This should be very consoling for any of you who are still grieving over the loss of someone you've loved. Jesus has felt what you feel! He knows—from inside—just what it's like to experience the death of someone you love.

In the gospel scene, Jesus and Martha speak briefly. Martha says she believes in a final resurrection on the last day. The Jewish people had not believed in the resurrection from the dead, but by Martha's time, it was beginning to work its way into Jewish faith. But Jesus was not interested in talking to her about the resurrection on the last day, as true as that is.

Instead, the message of Jesus to Martha comes down to this. "Martha, I am the Resurrection and the Life now. I can bring the dead to life now. I can give you a whole new way of life right now! Not just sometime later! Martha, the really important thing is not only to rise from the dead in fifty, or a hundred, or a thousand years from now—but to live and rise NOW! Do you believe this?"

The key to hearing this promise of life is in that question: "Do you believe this?" Not believe with your intellect. This kind of belief is not an assent to an idea, or to a theological statement. The word "believe" here has the sense of ultimate trust. Do you trust that God is the God of the living and not of the dead? Do you trust that out of the hopelessness and futility of the valley of dry bones, God can re-create new life?

Both Scripture stories today are about life, and they're about life now! And both Scripture stories are about ourselves. For too often we're dead in our sinful ways or in our inertia. We feel dead because of broken relationships, disillusionments, chronic illness. And we feel hopeless. And then the voice of Martha sounds within us: "It's too late. Nothing can be done about it now."

And so, it's very important—truly a matter of life or death—to be able to hear another voice as well, a voice reassuring us that nothing is ever too late for God! Because God the Creator is always re-creating, and renewing. And God's message is always: "You shall live! You shall not die!" But do you believe that?

PALM SUNDAY

First Reading: Isaiah 50:4–7
Responsorial Psalm: 22
Second Reading: Philippians 2:6–11
Gospel: Matthew 26:14—27:66 or 27:11–54

Today, with the Christian Church throughout the world, we enter into the final week of preparation for the great feast of Easter. Every year on Palm Sunday, we hear one of the Gospel accounts of the passion and death of Christ. This year, the account of the passion of Christ that we will hear sung by our choir is from the Gospel of Matthew.

I urge you to listen very carefully, as if for the first time. It could well be that some of what you hear will strike you with a new clarity and power. We will kneel for a few moments of respectful silence after the mention of the death of the Lord.

So let us listen to Matthew's telling of the great and terrible and wonderful story of the passion of Jesus.

Whenever our patron saint, Ignatius Loyola, led someone in prayer over the events of Holy Week, he asked that I be very much aware that Jesus is going to his suffering and death *for me, for my sins, and for my sake!* The greatest value you and I can set on the passion and death of Christ is to believe this. And then to allow that belief to truly impact the way I live…and the way I die. Today, with the Christian Church throughout the world, we enter into the final week of preparation for the great Feast of Easter.

After a long and rich Scripture reading like this, I think what we really need is time to absorb it. Hearing a reading of the Passion is like walking into the Sistine Chapel and looking up. There's simply too much to take in in one visit! We will re-visit the Passion this Friday as we listen to St. John's version of those last hours in Christ's life.

Suffering and tragedy are unfortunately part of life, and we often wonder where the loving God is when we're confronted by it. The Church gives us this passion narrative today so that all our own stories of pain and suffering can find meaning. I'm sure you've had suffering of your own, and surely you hear about the tragedies and pain of others, that challenge your faith in God's love and providence. This is especially so when it's the innocent who suffer. And God knows there are too many innocents suffering in our world today.

How do we deal with such a dark mystery?

As Christians, we must do whatever we can to alleviate suffering wherever we find it—with the conviction that God does not inflict suffering, and that the Jesus of the Gospels is always shown curing it when he meets it.

There will be many times in our life when I think the only way we can deal with suffering is by contemplating Christ crucified. By taking a crucifix in our hands and simply holding it there. There is no need to speak. Simply keep gazing at it silently with reverence and awe.

And realize that this man was completely innocent, completely undeserving of any of this! And that he endured all of it willingly, with full consent, so as to thoroughly bond with us in our own suffering and dying.

What his horrible death is telling us is that our loving God has taken upon himself all our afflictions, all our individual and communal stories of pain. And in those sufferings, he is ONE with us. Through all the events of his passion, he's saying to us: I have not come to take AWAY your sufferings, but to *share* them with you.

This is the great mystery we're contemplating this week.

SEASON OF
EASTER

EASTER SUNDAY

First Reading: Acts 10:34a, 37–43
Responsorial Psalm: 118
Second Reading: Colossians 3:1–4 or 1 Corinthians 5:6b–8
Gospel: John 20:1–9

❧

I speak for all of us on the staff here at St. Ignatius when I wish each of you a very happy and blessed Easter! For secular and commercial America, Easter is a celebration of the arrival of Spring. If you go into a card store looking for an Easter card, most of the cards you find are cards with colorful bunnies on them, in a field of bright flowers, carrying baskets of colored eggs, and singing "Happy Easter!" "Happy Spring!" The cards are cheerful. They're light-hearted. And they're very pagan.

For Christians, today is a celebration of life! But in a far deeper sense than the return of sunlight and green grass and spring flowers.

What we dare claim today is that life is permanent. It does not end in death and decay. We are not made for death and decay!

It is our faith that on that first Easter, God the Father brought Jesus back from the dead. This really happened! It's not a story the apostles made up.

It was not a dream, and Jesus was not a ghost. He had a real body they could see and touch.

The early Church was built on this foundation. The resurrection is the only major teaching of the Church that was never debated by the bishops of the Church, or by an ecumenical council of the Church…and there have been twenty-one councils in the two-thousand-year history of the Church. There was no need for debate on the historicity of the resurrection.

Because if Christ had not risen from the dead, there would be no Church. No bishops. No ecumenical councils—no Christians! And we wouldn't be here.

In fact, if Jesus had not risen from the dead, we would know precious little about him. He would have been one among the many holy prophets in Jewish history.

St. Paul has some very strong words to say about this to the Christian community at Corinth: "If Christ has not been raised from the dead, then we have nothing to preach, and you have nothing to believe…If our hope in Christ is good for this life only and no more, then we deserve more pity than anyone else in all the world."

(That's St. Paul in his First Letter to the Corinthians, chapter 15, verses 14 and 19, alt. translation.)

At this time of year, I'm reminded of a film I saw several years ago about the life of Jesus. Some of you may have seen it. It's called The Last Temptation of Christ, based on a novel by the Greek writer, Nikos Kazantzakis, and directed by Martin Scorsese. There's one scene in the film that stands out in my memory—the scene of the raising of Lazarus from the dead. After the stone is rolled away from the tomb, Jesus cries out loudly: "Lazarus, come out!" (John 11:43).

But nothing happens. So, Jesus draws closer to the opening of the tomb and falls to his knees in prayer. And suddenly, a hand comes forth from the tomb. Jesus reaches in and takes hold of the hand.

The dead man seems to be pulling Jesus into the darkness of the tomb. But Jesus rallies and pulls Lazarus out. Lazarus is ashen white, and covered with dirt, but he's alive! It's a thrilling moment!

The power of Jesus over death was real and visible to all who were gathered there that day.

Easter Sunday

This is what we celebrate today. We celebrate the immense power of God's love! And we have intimations of this power in our experience of human love.

Love always exacts a price because it involves the real possibility of losing the one we love in death. And all our human instincts cry out against that! To lose someone you love in death is heartbreaking. And we have an inbuilt rebellion against it.

This revulsion we feel toward death is a powerful sign from God! It's a sign that there's more to life's story than the separation and finality of death.

For when love is very powerful—when love is God himself—there's no way death can have the final word. If God were powerless in the face of death, then death would be the real power behind the world—the real God.

Because, in the end, all the beauty and goodness of life—in the unselfish acts of kindness people do for one another—all that would be a sham. Because it would all come to nothing.

The reason to send a greeting card today is not because Spring is here, but because we are loved by a mighty God! And this love is stronger than death! This is the truth the divine lover invites us to believe with our whole heart and mind!

This is why we celebrate today—even in the face of the ominous darkness and brutality and war that unnerves so much of our world this Easter day. Despite that darkness—and despite the pain and death that comes with it—the one recurring word we will hear in all the Masses for the next seven weeks is the word: "*Alleluia!*"

Alleluia! Life, not death, triumphs!

A blessed Easter to you all!

SECOND SUNDAY
OF EASTER

First Reading: Acts 2:42–47
Responsorial Psalm: 118
Second Reading: 1 Peter 1:3–9
Gospel: John 20:19–31

In this Gospel today, it's still Easter Sunday! It's evening, and the eleven apostles are hiding out together in one room—with the doors shut and locked. Earlier that day, Mary Magdalene had come rushing in with great joy and amazement, and told them she had seen the Lord, and that he was alive! You would think a giant party would have started then at such news! You might think the disciples would run out into the streets to shout the good news for everyone to hear! But no, they didn't budge out of that locked room. They were filled with fear. Afraid of the people who had killed Jesus. And afraid for their own uncertain future. What will happen to us now? Where will we go? How will we live?

And as they're thinking such thoughts, Jesus suddenly appears and stands there. He's not stopped by the doors we lock out of fear or anxiety. He comes as he always comes, speaking peace to them! And he comes as always, bearing the marks of suffering and death on his body.

I'm glad Thomas was not with them when this happened! I'm

glad he missed that first meeting, and that he wasn't convinced by just the words of those excited, overjoyed disciples. Like so many of us, Thomas wanted evidence. He wanted to see for himself what the others saw. I'm glad for that reaction!

And I'm even happier that the risen Jesus made that second visit, just to help Thomas work through his doubts and arrive at faith. And I suspect the early Church, instead of criticizing Thomas for his weak faith, saw this story as a real treasure! For we have to remember that by the time this Gospel was written in the late first century, eyewitnesses to Christ's resurrection appearances were dying out. And people were being asked to believe in Christ not only without having seen him, but without having seen those who had. So here, in this meeting with Jesus today, Thomas becomes a symbol of the growing Church that's asked to believe what it has not seen.

So, it seems John writes about this meeting not just for the Church of his time, but for the Church in every generation since. Because for Christians from the second century to this day, to have faith means to believe without seeing. Thomas didn't want faith at that moment. He wanted vision. That's a luxury he could have that we can't have. For us to believe is to believe in the dark. We have some light. We have enough light to be able to make our way, but not enough light to clear things up.

There will always be questions. What will life after death be like? What will a resurrected body be like? We'd like to know. We have our doubts. There is a Thomas in us all! And he's a reminder that questions and doubts are by no means hostile to faith. Too often we're victims of the myth that says faith means not asking any questions. Not so! In fact, questioning what others tell us, and what has been handed down to us and passively received, may be the only way that real and lasting faith is born. Faith can never prosper by pretending that there are no problems.

And so, doubting and questioning shouldn't be a source of great worry or anxiety for us. Because more likely, doubts are a sign that we care! And they are a sign that we're thinking! Doubts don't have to mean we're losing our faith. More often, they mean we're disappointed because we don't understand things better.

So, if you have religious doubts now and then, welcome to the real world of adult Christians. I'm sure there have been times when you've doubted you were making the right business decision, or career change, or the right decision as to how to deal with your children in bringing them up. And yet I'm sure, in spite of these doubts, you continued doing business. And you kept on parenting your children and did your very best for them.

One final thought this morning. You notice in the story that Thomas looks for faith within the community of the disciples. He doesn't leave them. He doesn't bolt! And they don't exclude him because he dares to doubt! This is an important point. And you notice that it's to the community that Jesus comes to give Thomas the opportunity to resolve his doubts.

This means the Church should always be a community where people are searching for greater understanding, and where questions are welcomed and honored. We need a climate in the Church in which questioners and doubters are allowed to speak. Where they're not silenced or driven away.

I suspect maybe Thomas is going to take a beating in some pulpits around the world today! Stubborn, questioning, doubting Thomas. Wanting to experience Christ for himself, not simply on the word of others. But that's not all that bad. And I suspect there are many Thomases among us here this morning. May our faith in Jesus deepen! And, in the end, may our faith give way to vision—in seeing him for ourselves!

THIRD SUNDAY
OF EASTER

First Reading: Acts 2:14, 22–33
Responsorial Psalm: 16
Second Reading: 1 Peter 1:17–21
Gospel: Luke 24:13–35

❦

If it weren't written in the New Testament, the story we just heard is the kind of story you would hope to find as you read through the Gospels. Imagine being on a walk and having Jesus come along and join you on your walk! He is so interested in you as he strolls along with you in easy conversation. There's something deep within us that craves this kind of personal contact with the Lord!

The two disciples trudging away from Jerusalem in today's story have had their dreams shattered. They had expectations of a powerful Messiah who would liberate the Jewish people from their Roman conquerors. They dreamt of a Messiah who would set up his own glorious kingdom, a kingdom foretold so repeatedly by the Old Testament prophets.

But Jesus failed miserably to meet that expectation. He got himself killed, and he hadn't made a single dent in the political situation in Palestine!

"We were hoping," the two confess to one another. We were hoping! Some of the saddest words a person can speak. In essence, they are saying: "We were hoping he was the one. We believed things might really change, but we were wrong."

And it's over now, as they walk the road that leads away from Jerusalem. I think everyone has walked this road at one time or another. It's the road you walk when you've lost your job or when a loved one has died. It's the road of deep disappointment.

They're surprised when a stranger joins them. And as he walks along with them, he begins to do what he characteristically loves to do. He brings light to their darkness. And he brings hope to their gloom.

He begins to explain to them every passage of the Hebrew Scriptures that referred to him. And their spirits soar! "Stay with us, for it is nearly evening," they beg him.

I think it's important to notice how Jesus brings the two of them to recognize him. At first, they hadn't recognized him at all. And this is quite typical. For God frequently goes unnoticed in our life, doesn't he?

Especially in times of distress. Where is God then? We had hoped God would rescue us, but God failed and didn't rescue us. We have no hint that God is present—now, with us.

That's why this Gospel this morning is such a treasure! Jesus comes to the disappointed. He comes to those who have given up. That makes this whole story a story about the blessing of brokenness.

And the Church, must show that same preference! I think the Church has done that through its social teachings that defend the rights and dignity of the broken and powerless in our world.

It's important to notice in this Gospel story today that what allows the two disciples to recognize Jesus is the experience he gives them of something very much like our Eucharist here today. While they're walking along, what happens is very similar to what goes on in the first part of every Mass. They listen to passages from Scripture, and Jesus gives them a kind of homily. Afterwards, when they get into the house and sit down at table, Jesus takes some bread, blesses it, breaks it, and gives it to them to eat—much like what happens in the second part of every Mass when we receive Holy Communion together.

But this begins to have meaning for the two disciples only in hindsight! Only after they had eaten the bread did they recognize who this was. And isn't this the way it often is with us? We think of times in our life that were difficult and painful. And years later, looking back, you say to yourself: "I wouldn't want to go through that again, but now I see there was a grace there. It was a painful time in my life, but God was with me. And there was unexpected good that came out of that pain."

This story has been saved by the Church to encourage us and remind us that we don't walk alone, and that it's OK to complain, and OK to talk about hopes that have been dashed.

But the story also promises us God's caring presence. And this is why we gather here. Because the hope is that we meet Jesus here! The hope is that Jesus becomes less of a stranger to us here! That by listening to the Word of God in Scripture, and by eating the bread of life that is his real presence, we will be nourished and strengthened for the journey that lies ahead of us.

This is the best reason I know for coming here Sunday after Sunday! In a very real sense, Jesus has caught up with us here! And this is the place he returns to meet us again and again, as we share the Word and break the bread.

FOURTH SUNDAY
OF EASTER

First Reading: Acts 2:14a, 36–41
Responsorial Psalm: 23
Second Reading: 1 Peter 2:20b–25
Gospel: John 10:1–10

The earliest ancestors of the Jewish people were nomads—owning no property, and not tied to any one location, but traveling with their flocks and herds wherever there was pastureland for the animals to graze on. They lived in a part of the world that has been very much in the news. They lived in what is now Iraq.

The Jewish people never forgot those origins. In the early books of the Hebrew Bible, they told the stories of major figures like Abraham, and Moses, and David—all of them shepherds caring for sheep. And long after most of them stopped being shepherds themselves, they pictured God as a shepherd—a shepherd guarding his flock with tender care.

This is the image of God that comes to us in the psalm today, and in the second reading from Peter, and in the tenth chapter of John's Gospel that we begin to hear this morning. In the words of the psalm: "The Lord is my shepherd, there is nothing I shall want."

This psalm is frequently read, or sung, at funeral Masses. Mourners can easily identify with it—especially with the verse that says: "If I should walk in the valley of darkness no evil would I fear, for you are there with your crook and your staff to give me comfort." Mourners can identify with this because that's where they are at that moment.

The psalm doesn't pretend that evil and death don't exist! Terrible things happen, and they happen to good people as well as to bad people. And death lies ahead for all of us. The author of the psalm doesn't try to explain evil or to minimize it. He simply says he will not fear evil! For all the power evil has, it doesn't have the power to make him afraid.

To say that "the Lord is my shepherd" is to say we won't have to face bad things alone! "For you are at my side," in the words of the psalm. You are with me. And this makes the world much less frightening.

Here in this part of the Gospel, Jesus is not just the Good Shepherd. He also identifies himself as "The Gate" to the sheepfold. What on earth does that mean? I had to do a little research on this to understand what Jesus is getting at here.

A shepherd, at the end of the day, had to gather his sheep into an enclosure—into a sheepfold—to protect them and keep them together for the night. The enclosure was made by stacking up rocks, and forming a kind of pen where the sheep would be guarded from predatory animals. It had a single opening for the sheep to pass through. And once the sheep were all in, the shepherd would lie down across the opening. He becomes the gate to the sheepfold so that nothing can get through without going over his body first. Without confronting him, or even killing him, first.

And that image of Jesus as the gate, as the door, calls to mind another meaning.

It's not only physically that people can be locked in. We can be trapped in so many ways! By sickness, by the things we own, by an addiction. By a deep-seated anger toward someone who has hurt us. All these things can lock us up, and lock us in. We don't know what to do, or how to escape. There's no exit, no gate, no door.

And then there's that man from Nazareth who says this morning: "I am the door!"

So many people in our world today face things they think won't change. So many feel desperate, without an escape hatch. And then a Gospel like this comes along. And we hear Jesus say: "I am the door. I am the door." I can lead you out! I can lead you out—into peace, and a fuller life. Come through me!

If only our world would hear this message today! If only our world would find the door to life and peace in our times!

FIFTH SUNDAY OF EASTER

First Reading: Acts 6:1–7
Responsorial Psalm: 33
Second Reading: 1 Peter 2:4–9
Gospel: John 14:1–12

✲

W e know that each of the Sundays after Easter is a celebration of Easter all over again! Easter Day itself is not enough. And so, we have seven Sundays in the Easter Season. Today we hear Jesus make one of the great Easter promises.

You probably recognize this Gospel today as part of the last meal Jesus had with his friends the night before his death. It's a goodbye meal, and they're understandably distressed. They're afraid they'll be left to fend for themselves without the security of the daily and familiar life they had with Jesus. We hear Jesus respond to their fear with one of the great promises of Easter.

"I am going to prepare a place for you," he tells them. And then "I will come back again and take you to myself, so that where I am you also may be."

We interpret these words correctly as a promise of eternal life and heaven. But we have a hard time with heaven. Where is it, anyway? What will it be like? It's almost impossible to imagine! Besides, all our guesses about what heaven will be like are influenced by our human categories. We can't help but think of a future life except in terms of what we experience here and now in time and space. And so, the questions we sometimes ask are predictable.

"How old will I be in the next life?"
"Will I be the same age as when I die?"
"Will there be marriage in heaven?"
"Will I know my loved ones."

Our experience of this life isn't much help in trying to imagine a future life that will be quite different. Yet I think we can be helped by an analogy. Let's suppose you are a fetus about to be born. You know what life has been like for you these past nine months, and you wonder if there could be life beyond the womb that has been so familiar and secure for you. It seems impossible! Because once the cord is cut, the means of sustaining life will be gone. How can you exist then? This is what you can't imagine!

Now let's suppose that a fetus who has escaped the womb to the other side of life comes back and speaks to you.

"I know you have a wonderful life here," the newborn tells you. "But this is only a preparation! In a short time, you'll be in the light! You'll eat through your mouth and breathe air! Your arms and legs will do more things than you could ever imagine now—with all your kicking and swimming around!"

Now a fetus in the womb wouldn't be able to understand any of that. Life in the outside world is completely incomprehensible to an unborn child. And I think it's the same with us with respect to eternal life. What heaven will be like, we simply can't know! I'm reminded of what St. Paul writes in his First Letter to the Corinthians: "No eye has seen, no ear has heard, no human heart has conceived, what God has prepared for those who love him" (1 Corinthians 2:9, NRSV).

Heaven is far beyond what we can imagine! And this can be frightening!

The best remedy for the fear of death and dying is a deep faith in the words we hear Jesus speak today. "I am going to prepare a place for you...and then I will come back again and take you to myself so that where I am you also may be."

That's the great promise through all the pages of the Bible and too often we don't hear it. God says over and over again: "I am with you."

So frequently is this the message of Scripture that we can describe and define God in these very words! Who is God? God is "the one who is with me."

Let me tell you a favorite story that may help drive this home. There's an American Indian legend about a tribe from the Great Lakes region that had a tradition of sacrificing—every year—one of the young unmarried women to the great god of the waters who they feared very much. Their practice was to draw lots, and the woman selected was put into a canoe in the river above Niagara Falls and ordered to go over the Falls as a human sacrifice. This one year the daughter of the chief of the tribe was the one who drew the lot. When the day came for her to go over the Falls, the chief couldn't be found to preside over the ceremony. The tribe began to complain that he couldn't be trusted any longer to fulfill his responsibilities as chief. So, they went ahead with the ceremony without him.

They put his daughter into a canoe and pushed it out into the river. And as they were doing that, they saw another canoe coming onto the river out of the bushes where it had been concealed. And they recognized the person in the canoe was their chief, the girl's father. And then, suddenly, both canoes were caught in a fast-moving current, and they went over the Falls together—father and daughter, together.

This is only a legend, of course, but it has a message that's critically important and needs to be heard. It's the message of Jesus in the Gospel today: "I will take you with me on the journey. I will be with you, alongside you. You have nothing to fear!"

SIXTH SUNDAY OF EASTER

First Reading: Acts 8:5–8, 14–17
Responsorial Psalm: 66
Second Reading: 1 Peter 3:15–18
Gospel: John 14:15–21

🌿

The fear of abandonment may be one of our most basic anxieties. Here in this Gospel, on the night before his death, and during their last meal together, Jesus is concerned about the effect his death is going to have on his closest friends. He wants to assure them that he's not going to abandon them to their own resources. His conversation is of giving himself back to them—in another way. He's going to leave them with something more than just a memory. And so, he promises to send them what John's Gospel today calls an "Advocate."

Advocate is a legal term meaning someone who pleads for you on your behalf. A kind of defense attorney, who will stand at your side to help you in need, and offer you guidance and support. Jesus himself has been their Advocate, and now, he says, he'll send "another Advocate"—identified a few verses later as the Holy Spirit.

Every Sunday, during the recitation of the Creed, we say: "I believe in the Holy Spirit, the Lord, the giver of life, who proceeds from the Father and the Son." Belief in this Holy Spirit is foundational to our faith...one of the nonnegotiables! And yet the Holy Spirit can be a problem for us! We don't know the Spirit the way we know the Father and the Son. Of the three persons in the Trinity, the Spirit is the hardest to pin down. Most of us can at least begin to describe the Father and the Son. But God the Holy Spirit?

One of the best understandings of who this Holy Spirit, this "Advocate," is was given by the great New Testament scholar, the late Raymond Brown. He spoke of the Holy Spirit as "the presence of Jesus while Jesus is absent," or "the presence of Jesus after Jesus' return to the Father."

Let me repeat that again, because it's so important. The Holy Spirit is "The presence of Jesus while Jesus is with the Father."

Jesus never intended to leave his disciples to their own resources. And he had frequently told them that. He had frequently promised them: "I am with you always." That promise becomes powerfully realized at the first Pentecost which we commemorate two weeks from today. The coming of the Holy Spirit to the apostles on that first Pentecost was like another Incarnation of God in the world, a second birth of Christ as it were, and it brought phenomenal life and growth to the early Church.

The felt presence of the Holy Spirit in the life of the Church was the reason why there's no sign in the New Testament of longing for the "good old days" when Jesus was physically present. There's no nostalgia in the New Testament. No hankering to go back to a better time!

And there's very good reason for that. Because the early Christians never felt that Jesus had left them! He was not physically present, but he was present in a new way, in the Holy Spirit living within the Church. "I will not leave you orphans. I will come to you" is what we're promised here in today's Gospel.

With the coming of the Holy Spirit to them, the early Christians will not have to rely on their limited memory of Jesus. Instead, the Spirit will be a living presence, ever responsive to the new situations they will have to face. In a way, Jesus was saying: You don't know everything yet. You have more to learn. In every generation you'll be faced with new questions and problems. "The Spirit will be your teacher," he tells them a little later on that evening (John 14:26). "The Spirit will guide you into all the truth" (John 16:13).

The Church began with a dozen very simple men and the wildly improbable story that a man put to death by his own people as a criminal was God himself. They started out preaching a way of life that challenged almost every standard of the world around them. And in its two-thousand-year history, the Church has survived enormous obstacles: persecutions, schisms, heresies, scandals. We've survived tyrannical governments and bad popes. You may know that Dante, in his *Divine Comedy*, put two popes in his *Inferno*!

There's been no period in its history, except briefly in the Middle Ages, when the Church enjoyed real tranquility. By all human rules, we can say that the Church should have died many times over! And yet, today, the Church is very much alive and growing, numbering over a billion members, in every corner of the world!

When Pope St. John Paul the Second died, there was much speculation about who would succeed him as pope. Peter Steinfels was the religion editor for *The New York Times* in those days, and in one of his columns he recalled that a high-ranking Vatican official was asked in an interview whether "the Holy Spirit plays a role in the election of the pope."

The Vatican official replied: "I would not say so in the sense that the Holy Spirit picks out the pope, because there are too many contrary instances of popes the Holy Spirit would obviously not have picked."

"The Spirit's role should be understood in a much more elastic sense," he said. "Probably the only assurance the Spirit offers is that the thing cannot be totally ruined."

The Vatican official being interviewed was Cardinal Joseph Ratzinger, who himself became the next pope! What he was saying here is that the Church is going to survive—no matter WHO is elected pope.

Sixth Sunday of Easter

In almost every verse of today's Gospel, Jesus assures the infant Church that it will never be left on its own. No matter how bad it gets, or how seriously you mess up, I will not abandon you. I will not leave you orphans. I will come to you.

This is why we take seven weeks to celebrate Easter—seven weeks filled with Alleluias!

SEVENTH SUNDAY
OF EASTER[1]

First Reading: Acts 1:12–14
Responsorial Psalm: 27
Second Reading: 1 Peter 4:13–16
Gospel: John 17:1–11a

Have you ever wondered how Jesus prayed? Have you ever wondered what he prayed about? What his concerns were? Well, we get some idea of that in the prayer that has come down to us as the "Lord's Prayer"—the "Our Father"—the prayer Jesus taught his disciples when they came to him and asked him how to pray.

We also get an answer to how Jesus prayed in the chapter of John's Gospel we begin to hear today, chapter 17. This is still part of the conversation he had with the twelve at their last supper together, the night before his execution. One of the things you notice in the part of the prayer we're hearing tonight is how very personal and intimate that prayer is. The words Jesus uses most frequently as he

---

1. See "Holy Days of Obligation" in Liturgical Year C for The Ascension of the Lord. In certain dioceses in the United States, the Ascension is transferred to the Seventh Sunday of Easter, displacing these readings.

speaks to the Father are the words: "You" and "Me." Or, "You" and "I." Or "Mine" and "Yours."

It's reassuring to hear that Jesus was praying for himself! So often, my own concerns are the things I pray about. And that's OK! In many parts of the New Testament, we're encouraged to pray for our own needs. What's not so good is if that's all I ever pray about. If all I talk to God about is me, I'm being very self-absorbed.

But you notice in this prayer of Jesus that he soon moves away from words like "me" and "I" and "mine"—to the words "them" and "they." And for a longer while, Jesus prays to the Father about his apostles. Understandably, he's deeply concerned about leaving them. He's concerned for their welfare and their future.

And then, toward the end of his prayer—a part not given in our Gospel reading today—Jesus prays for all those who will come to believe in him. He moves beyond the circle of his disciples and begins to pray for us all!

We learn a lot about prayer from this prayer of Jesus to his Father in the seventeenth chapter of John's Gospel.

For one thing, we learn prayer is not thinking about God. If I'm thinking about you, you're the focal point of my thoughts. But that's not communication with you. Prayer is communication with God. I don't think about God. I talk to God. I let God know who I am, and what my hopes and concerns are.

I think the prayer we overhear Jesus praying tonight is a strong encouragement to be very plain and direct with God in prayer, and to speak in a familiar way with God, not in any formal or distant way, but as one friend speaks to another—as St. Ignatius always would say! We don't have to feel we have to be ceremonious with God when we come to prayer. What's best is to be totally yourself with God, and go to Him exactly as you are, and as you are now—without being artificial, and without trying to disguise your inner feelings.

The psalms are good examples of this kind of simple, unaffected prayer. There are 150 psalms in the Old Testament. All of them are prayers dating to at least a thousand years before the birth of Christ. They were prayers that Jesus himself knew and quotes from. And they cover a wide range of human emotions.

Psalm 42 is a psalm of longing for God in the midst of discouragement and questioning. Psalm 104 praises God for the beauties of creation. Psalm 23 is a psalm of trust in God—even at a dark time in life. Psalm 13 pleads angrily with God: "How long, O Lord? Will you forget me forever?" (NRSV).

The authors of these psalms let it all hang out in prayer! They're completely transparent. There's no attempt to present only a good face to God. What's important is to be real before God— totally natural. God really wants to know everything about me— even my dark side and the things that seem so ungodly!

And isn't that what's expected between close friends?

PENTECOST

First Reading: Acts 2:1–11
Responsorial Psalm: 104
Second Reading: Corinthians 12:3b–7, 12–13
Gospel: John 20:19–23 or John 15:26–27; 16:12–15

💐

E xactly fifty days ago, we were celebrating Easter! And today we
bring the Easter Season to a close with this Feast of Pentecost.

Pentecost is one of the three great celebrations in the Church
year. It ranks with Christmas and Easter, though we probably don't
think of it that way. I'm sure you aren't going home to a special Pentecost dinner today as you might be on Christmas or Easter!

Pentecost is major because it commemorates a new coming
of God to the world on this day—a sort of second Christmas in a
sense, because God comes again, this time never to leave.

The Gospels tell us that after his resurrection and ascension,
Jesus left the world to be with the Father in glory. The last thing
he told his disciples before his ascension was to go back to Jerusalem and wait there for the fulfillment of God's promise that the
Holy Spirit would come to them. They had little or no idea what that
meant, but they went back to Jerusalem—not to the temple, but to
an ordinary room in an ordinary house. And there they waited.

And they prayed while they waited, but they didn't have to
wait long. On the day of Pentecost, a Jewish holy day that happened
every year—fifty days after Passover, they were all together in that

one room when they got a crash course in power. In Luke's telling of it in our first reading this morning, there was a sound of rushing, violent wind, and then there were beams of fire that came to rest on each one of them. They were "fired up," I guess you could say, and rushed out into the streets of Jerusalem, praising God and preaching to the people in the different foreign languages of the pilgrims who had come for the religious holiday from as far away as Rome and Egypt. Luke relates that three thousand people were baptized that day! That's almost four times the capacity of St. Ignatius Church!

What began that day spread like a forest fire! It spread across nations and across cultures. In thirty years, Christianity became so powerful that the Roman Emperor, Nero, made it the target of an all-out persecution.

A people who spoke not a word of Hebrew came to believe in a Hebrew Lord who is worshiped today in every language known to us!

All this happened by the power of God, the Holy Spirit.

The Greek word for power in the New Testament is *dunamis.* I mention this because we get some interesting English words from that Greek word. We get the words *dynamite, dynamic,* and *dynamo.* Pentecost was dynamite for the early Church. It got it going and has kept it going all these centuries despite the many crises that have threatened to bring it down.

The New Testament speaks of this Holy Spirit as the abiding presence of God with us. At their last meal together, Jesus had promised the apostles he would return to them. "I will not leave you orphans," he tells them. "I will come back to you" (John 14:18). It's words like these that have made one contemporary theologian Raymond Brown describe the Holy Spirit as "the personal presence of Jesus in the [world] while Jesus is with the Father."

But you might ask: how do we know that God's own self, the Holy Spirit, is really in the world and at work? St. Paul, in his Letter to the Galatians, speaks of nine ways the Holy Spirit characteristically works among us. Paul says that what the Holy Spirit brings is: "love, joy, peace, patience, kindness, generosity, faithfulness, gentleness, and self-control" (Galatians 5:22–23). Whenever we find ourselves more loving, or more generous, or more self-controlled, or more at peace within ourselves—or whenever we meet these qualities in other people, we know for sure that God the Holy Spirit is at work! We simply cannot produce these qualities on our own. They are gifts from God.

It is our faith that the Holy Spirit is active and at work in the Church now, and until the end of time! That is the promise Christ left us, and God is always faithful to God's promises. We never hear the Church saying: "Oh, wouldn't it be wonderful if we were back there again in those days when we could see Jesus, and hear him speak, and reach out to touch him." There's no nostalgia in the Church. Because Jesus has not left us alone. He is with us today through the Holy Spirit as truly as when he was physically among us.

On this Feast of Pentecost, which we sometimes refer to as the birthday of the Church, I want to leave you with words of love and admiration for the Church written by the late Fr. Walter Burghardt, a Jesuit theologian and gifted homilist, one of my seminary professors, who in the last years of his life was stationed at Georgetown University. He writes:

> In the course of a half century, I have seen more Christian corruption than you have read of. I have tasted it. I have been reasonably corrupt myself. And yet, I love this Church, this living, pulsing, sinning people of God. Why? For all the Christian hate, I experience here a community of love. For all the institutional idiocy, I see here a tradition of reason. For all the individual repressions, I breathe here an air of freedom. For all the fear of sex, I discover here the redemption of my body. In an age so inhuman, I touch here tears of compassion. In a world so grim, I share here rich joy. In the midst of death, I find

here an incomparable stress on life. For all the apparent absence of God, I sense here the real presence of Christ.

So, this is what this gifted theologian wrote! And this is what gives us reason today to be grateful. And reason to be confident for the future of the Church!

ORDINARY TIME

THE MOST
HOLY TRINITY
(Sunday after Pentecost)

First Reading: Exodus 34:4b–6, 8–9
Responsorial Psalm: Daniel 3
Second Reading: 2 Corinthians 13:11–13
Gospel: John 3:16—18

Our feast today of the Holy Trinity is about our Christian under-standing of God. It dares to speak about the inner nature of God—about who God is, in God's inner self. This is dangerous ter-ritory!

I heard a story one time about a priest who began his homily on Trinity Sunday with the words: "What we're celebrating today is a great mystery, and I have no words to add to that. Amen." Well, I might like to do that, too, but I won't. Because we do know some-thing about the mystery. There would be no point in God revealing mysteries to us unless there is at least some aspect of them that we can understand.

The mystery of God is that God is one God, but three distinct, separate persons.

But even as we say that, we have to admit the inadequacy of those words. Because three persons sounds dangerously like three individual entities, three single beings, three gods. Which is not what we want to say about God at all! St. Augustine wrote extensive reflections on the Trinity. Essentially, he said: "I know there are three in God. I don't know what to call them!"

We believe there will come a time when, in heaven, we will know God as God is. That's God's own promise to us. But until then, God is always beyond our comprehension! Because God transcends the human intellect and is inaccessible to it. And so infinitely outside the range of our best words and concepts.

We believe God revealed something of himself to the ancient Hebrews. And that the Hebrew Scriptures speak of God's actions in human history. But these same Scriptures insist that God is hidden and can't be grasped by the human mind, and can't be compared to a human person!

For Christians, this hidden, inaccessible God did the unthinkable. In today's Gospel, John says that "God so loved the world that he gave his only Son,...that the world might be saved through him." God became accessible, and visible, in Jesus Christ. We believe that Jesus is the human face of God! And this Jesus teaches us that God is Father, Son and Holy Spirit. The Church has always professed her faith in God in this triune way. And what this way is saying is that God is a community! A family!...of Father, Son, and Holy Spirit! This means God is not an "I" but a "We." Each divine person in the Trinity exists for the other two and shares everything with them.

Two weeks ago, we heard Jesus pray to his Father in John's Gospel. "All I have is yours," Jesus says in prayer to his Father, "And all you have is mine" (John 17:10, NJB). This is why the best understanding we have of God is given to us in John's first letter. "God is love," John writes (1 John 4:8). And this—better than anything else—defines God. God is love and nothing else but love!

And what we know about love is that it's relational. It's other directed, directed away from the self to another. That's the glory of love, that it's never static. It never stays within itself but goes out to the other!

And because we know this about God's inner nature—that

God is a loving, relational God, not alone and solitary—we have a great insight into our own human nature.

Sacred Scripture says that you and I are made in the image and likeness of God, right? It's not surprising, then, that we're meant to be in communion with one another. What makes us truly human is not a selfish life centered on me, but a shared life, involving you and me. We prosper and become fully human only through our relationships.

I have to say that again, because it's so important on this Feast of the Trinity. We prosper and become fully human only through our relationships.

Just think for a second about what have been the best moments of your life. Surely the best moments involve being in relationship.

For instance, when a parent hugs you, when your spouse embraces you, when your boss affirms you. When someone who cares for you is in the same room with you. When friendship is valuable and strong. We remember these as our best moments. And they were always moments when we were in relation with someone else. What's always a huge disappointment is when a very special moment comes along. You see a magnificent sunset, or a splendid falling star one night, and you're alone. You have no one to share it with!

There's something written in our very nature that says: You must be with. This is the way we're made. And that's what life is all about! Or to put it another way: life is about loving. It's about communion. That's how we come to fulfillment, to human completion.

We know when we're sick, for example, we want someone to be with us, someone who cares. Someone to acknowledge our sickness. Even people who are dying need to be in relationship. They're not so much afraid of death. They're afraid of dying alone!

One of the greatest human sufferings is loneliness. Because there's something deep in our nature that says: It's not good to be alone. You must be with. We know that in the penal system, what they do when they want to punish someone severely is that they put that person in solitary confinement. Short of death, that's the worst punishment. Because it's against human nature. And it's against God's nature. Because whatever else the Trinity means, it means relationship. It means communion. The God we know is a holy communion!

So, I think we have to be grateful for what today's feast tells us about God. And grateful, too, for what it tells us about ourselves. We have a desperate drive to be in relationship, and we're happiest when we are in relationship. Isn't that true?

When there's no love in your life, you're miserable! And when you're separated from those you love, life is barely tolerable! We can't abide *being* separated from those we love. And today's Feast of the Trinity gives us the reason why that's so.

Praised be this God—Father, Son, and Holy Spirit—totally one and totally for one another...even while their love for one another spills out to the entire created world!

THE MOST HOLY BODY AND BLOOD OF CHRIST
(Sunday after Trinity Sunday)

First Reading: Deuteronomy 8:2–3, 14b–16a
Responsorial Psalm: 147
Second Reading: 1 Corinthians 10:16–17
Gospel: John 6:51–58

There's a slogan that has been around the Public Health Community for years. And it's a good one! I'm thinking of the saying: "You are what you eat."

Curiously enough, that idea has been part of Christian theology since the early days of St. Augustine in the fourth century! Augustine said it about the very mystery we celebrate today—The Body of Christ in the Eucharist. Augustine says you *become* the Body of Christ by properly receiving Christ who comes in the disguise of bread and wine. And what a remarkable claim that is!

What we believe as Catholics is that the Eucharist is not just a symbol. It's not bread that's meant to fill us with pious thoughts about the bread Jesus broke with the apostles at their Last Supper.

"I am the living bread come down from heaven," Jesus says in John's Gospel today. "Whoever eats this bread will live forever. And the bread I will give is my flesh for the life of the world….unless you eat the flesh of the Son of Man and drink his blood, you do not have life within you."

Jesus is saying this, not to his disciples sitting around him taking in every word. He's saying this in the synagogue in Capernaum to a group of hostile Jews who are scandalized by what they hear! And they begin to grumble and argue among themselves: "How can this man give us his flesh to eat?"

They thought he was referring to his physical body and urging them to some form of cannibalism! In fact, first-century Romans spread rumors that Christians ate flesh and drank blood during their religious worship.

In the world of Jesus, "flesh and blood," or "body and blood," was a way of speaking of the whole person. He's telling them he will give them the gift of himself in the form of food and drink.

The whole living Jesus is present in both the bread and wine. This means if you drink from the cup only, and don't take the bread, as some do who are allergic to wheat, for example, you're receiving the whole person, the full reality of Jesus within you. What a radical and seemingly impossible claim that is! St. John writes that even some of Christ's own disciples found this teaching too hard to take and they gave up on him! They left him because of the Eucharist.

In our own time, there are many Christian denominations that don't believe in the real presence of Jesus in the Eucharist. They find that too difficult to accept. And we have to admit: it's almost too good to be true, isn't it? That we should have regular access to Jesus through something as unglamourous and ordinary as *food*. But this is telling us something very important.

We know that food and drink are necessary for life and nourishment. If we stop eating and drinking, we'll die within a short time. By coming as food, Jesus is saying—in effect: "Let me nourish you. Let me give you life. Let me help you to grow to full stature as a Christian. You need me for that to happen. I want to be *part* of you and share your humanity with you. As intimately as food and drink are united with your body, so would I be united with you." This is the understanding of Eucharist that has been central to our Catholic faith and practice since the very beginning.

Jesus risks a lot by coming to us as food and drink. Because people don't always appreciate what they're being served. They prefer something else. Some refuse to eat. Or they eat very irregularly. But Jesus takes the risk. And whenever anyone receives the Eucharist properly disposed, we take into our own bodies the risen, glorified body of Jesus.

In a sense, this becomes another Incarnation. God once again takes human flesh. And, this time, WE become his indwelling!

Who wouldn't want that?

SECOND SUNDAY IN
ORDINARY TIME

First Reading: Isaiah 49:3, 5–6
Responsorial Psalm: 40
Second Reading: 1 Corinthians 1:1–3
Gospel: John 1:29–34

❧

This Sunday, the Church is still lingering over the Baptism of Jesus—the feast we celebrated a week ago. We get a different slant on the Baptism today from St. John, who gives us John the Baptist's own recollections of what happened that day.

In a sense, the Christian Church has been slightly uncomfortable with the baptism of Jesus, and you can't miss that when you read the Gospels. Mark is brief and straightforward. We're simply told that Jesus was baptized by John in the Jordan, and that a voice was heard from heaven: "You are my beloved Son; with you I am well pleased" (Mark 1:11). Another approved translation of St. Mark's Gospel puts it this way: "You are my son, the Beloved; my favor rests on you" (NJB). Matthew elaborates on this by adding that John tried to talk Jesus out of being baptized. In Luke, we're told that Jesus was baptized, but Luke won't come out and say that it was John who did it. Then, today, John's Gospel is the most skittish of all. John says he saw the Spirit descend like a dove upon Jesus, but he doesn't mention anything about a baptism at all! So you see, the Gospel writers sensed that there was a bit of a problem here. And the problem centers around why this happened in the first place. Why ever did Jesus get himself baptized? John's baptism was a baptism of repentance for sins, a sign of inner sorrow for personal sins committed. Surely, Jesus had no sins to be sorry about!

He might have stood on the shore and offered words of encouragement to those going into the water. But there was no reason for him to go in himself. We have to conclude that he gets into the water with all those sinners, not because he had to, but because he wanted to. He wanted to identify as closely as possible with sinful, flawed human beings. What a delight it is to see Jesus standing on the mud floor of the river and getting God's approval for doing that!

It was an extraordinary moment for him and a turning point in his adult life. Something happened at his Baptism that changed his life forever. After this, he no longer goes back to being the carpenter in Nazareth. He leaves behind the hidden, private life he had in a small town in northern Palestine, and launches out into the much broader world of the whole of Palestine. He takes his first giant step along the road "of his Father's business," as he called it years before, when he was a boy of 12 and was found in the temple in Jerusalem after he had been missing for three days.

What happened at his baptism involved an extraordinary experience of being loved by his Father. Surely Jesus knew before his baptism that his Father loved him. But at his baptism he learns it again in a new way—as a mature adult.

He feels deeply loved that day, and from then on, his life is different. It's redirected. He begins the most active and involved years of his life.

I want to dwell on this today because I'm convinced that God wants you and me to have this experience too—of feeling loved and accepted for who we are. Most of us think we have to win God's love. Most of us think we have to change before God will love us. The truth is: God loves us not because of anything we've done to earn that love, but because God is so loving and freely gives that love whether we deserve it or not! That's a very unfamiliar notion for us. We grow up inclined to see our whole existence in terms of quid pro quo. We assume people will be nice to us if we're nice to them. That they will help us if we help them. That they will love us if we love them. And so, we have this deeply rooted conviction that being loved is something you have to earn. In the practical and pragmatic world we live in, we can hardly imagine getting something for nothing. Everything has to be worked for!

And then we transfer this kind of thinking to our relationship with God. We think we have to earn God's love before God will love us.

When Jesus was baptized, three of the four Gospel writers tell us that the message he heard from the Father that day was this: "You are my beloved. It gives me great pleasure to look upon you." No words in Scripture are more beautiful than these! And we would love to hear these words addressed to ourselves. Who wouldn't want to know that God looks fondly upon us, that God is aware of our existence and cares about us? Who wouldn't be moved in knowing that we give God great pleasure, and that God loves us for who we are, and for what we are? I think we're desperate for this kind of love. And if we're fortunate, we receive it—on a human level—from at least some. Let me quote to you from someone who tells about an experience of feeling loved. He says:

> I was a neurotic for years. I was anxious and depressed and selfish. And everyone kept telling me to change. Everyone kept telling me how neurotic I was. And I resented them. And I agreed with them. And I wanted to change. But I couldn't bring myself to change, no matter how hard I tried.
>
> What hurt me the most was that my best friend kept telling me how neurotic I was and kept insisting that I change. And I agreed. But I felt powerless and trapped. Then one day my friend said to me: "Don't change. Stay as you are. It really doesn't matter whether you change or not. I love you just as you are." These words sounded

like music to my ears! "Don't change. Don't change. I
love you as you are." And I relaxed! And I came alive!
And something marvelous happened. I changed! Now I
know that I couldn't really change until I found someone
who would love me whether I changed or not. (Anthony
de Mello, *The Song of the Bird*)

I think this is a wonderful disclosure of how someone came
to a marvelous discovery that redirected his life. And I think this is
the good news of the Christian revelation. The words Jesus heard at
his baptism: "You are my beloved. It gives me great pleasure to look
upon you," are words spoken not just to Jesus, but indeed to each
of us as well. God does not pick and choose: "I will love this one,
but not that one." God is absolute love and can love only absolutely,
that is, without restriction. God looks upon us and finds each of us
utterly lovable. If you haven't gotten this message from hearing the
New Testament, you've missed the one really big message of the
Christian revelation!

That's why I'm glad the Church is lingering today over last
week's Feast of the Baptism of the Lord when he hears those wonderful words: "You are my beloved. It gives me great pleasure to
look upon you." Whenever you feel let down, I suggest you remember these words: "You are my beloved. It gives me great pleasure
to look upon you." When you feel like you're stuck, in mud, remind
yourself that you are God's beloved, and that nothing is ever going
to change that! Life is full of promise because God takes delight in
just looking at you.

THIRD SUNDAY IN ORDINARY TIME

First Reading: Isaiah 8:23–9:3
Responsorial Psalm: 27
Second Reading: 1 Corinthians 1:10–13, 17
Gospel: Matthew 4:12–23 or 4:12–17

❧

Here we are, at the end of the first month in the new calendar year, and well into the new Church liturgical year as well. And already we've had a sense of something new happening. The Gospels of the past two Sundays speak of the Baptism of Jesus—the one big event of his young adult life. That Baptism turned his life around—from the hidden life of a carpenter in the small town of Nazareth, to the very public life of an itinerant preacher and healer. After his Baptism, one of the first questions he had to decide, as he began those three brief years of public ministry, was where he was going to live and work. It's a decision many young adults have to grapple with.

He makes a surprising decision! You might think he would have chosen to settle somewhere near Jerusalem. After all, Jerusalem was the religious center of Judaism since the time of King David. It was the site of the temple, and the home of the great Jewish prophets like Isaiah, and Jeremiah, and Ezekiel. But no. Jesus heads to Capernaum, to the north of Nazareth, right on the Sea of Galilee.

Capernaum was part of the territory once occupied by the Jewish tribe of Naphtali. So, by settling there in Capernaum, Jesus is fulfilling the prophecy of Isaiah in our first reading today, and repeated in the Gospel: "The people who walked in darkness have seen a great light. Upon those who dwelt in the land of gloom, a light has shone." Jesus is that great light foretold by Isaiah.

If you were to visit the ruins of Capernaum today, the first thing you'd see as you approached is a simple sign hanging on a gate. The sign reads: "The town of Jesus." This was home for him. And it's not hard to see why Jesus settled here. Northern Galilee, with its lush and fertile land, was densely populated. And it had lots of traffic from different directions. The major roads of the ancient world—like the road from Damascus to Egypt— passed through here. A great mix of people lived here in Capernaum. There were Jews and non-Jews, many non-Jews coming from close by—from Samaria, and from what is now Syria and Lebanon. "Galilee of the Gentiles" it's called in the prophecy from Isaiah today. Living in Capernaum presented a unique opportunity for meeting and influencing all kinds of people.

Jesus would never again return to live in Nazareth where he had been brought up. The Gospels tell us he was not well received there—even by the people who knew him well. In contrast, we're told the people in the Capernaum area received him favorably.

They were an open-minded people by disposition and circumstances—more receptive to new ideas, new influences, new faces. Galilee could not keep new ideas out. And Jesus could work better in that environment. Because he was about something new. He was a different breed of prophet than the Jewish prophets who preceded him. And his message contained new developments beyond traditional Jewish theology. This would prove to be his downfall in a few short years, but at least—as he was beginning his active years of ministry—he wanted to live among people who would be receptive and open enough to give him a hearing.

The one recurring message people had to be open to hear is the message we hear him give today: "Repent, for the kingdom of heaven is at hand." There's another approved translation of those words that I like better. In that translation Jesus says: "You must change your hearts and minds, for the kingdom of heaven is at hand." I think this is the better translation because it makes it clear that change is at the very heart of repentance!

I want to speak to you for a few moments about change. It's a frequent Gospel imperative.

We must be open to change. We really must! It's the only way human growth can happen. And yet, most of us, I suspect, really don't like change all that much. We get very comfortable with routine. We like situations that are predictable. And yet we know life is not that way. I've always liked the saying of Cardinal John Henry Newman that "to live is to change, and to be perfect is to have changed often."

God is often behind change because God is always creating something new. We see that happening in our own bodies. Our bodies are being constantly renewed.

A biologist will tell you the human body is made up of three trillion cells, and that those cells are always dying and being replaced by new cells. Cancer is an example of what happens when cells don't die.

So, life means change! And what God has promised us is that God is actively at work in the changes that take place. In the Gospel this past Monday, Jesus is questioned as to why he and his disciples don't fast when the disciples of John the Baptist and the Pharisees do fast. The religious tradition of Israel had a long history of fasting on certain days of the week.

Jesus answers that one doesn't fast at a wedding feast. It wouldn't be appropriate for his disciples to fast while he was with them. Nor would it be appropriate to pour new wine into old, dried out wineskins, he tells them. The skins would burst, and the wine would be lost. New wine demands new wineskins!

Third Sunday in Ordinary Time

It's fair to say that the good news preached by Jesus in the Scriptures is always itself new wine! For every old situation in life, whether it be our stale marriages, or our compulsive habits and addictions, or our attachment to status and possessions—whatever!—the Gospel good news is that it's possible, with God's help, that all things can become new!

There's a wonderful pair of verses (18 and 19) in the prophet Isaiah, chapter 43, that reads: "No need to recall the past. No need to think about what was done before. See, I am doing a new thing! Can you not see it?" (NJB). This applies to the Church, as well as to individual persons like ourselves. Christianity can never be a settled or fixed thing. If that were to happen it would no longer be alive. The most settled things are in the graveyard. Anything alive is moving, and changing, and growing! I'm reminded of the remark of G.K. Chesterton, the British author and convert to Catholicism, that

> in a century or two spiritualism may be a tradition, and socialism may be a tradition, and Christian Science may be a tradition. But Catholicism will not be a tradition. It will still be a nuisance—and a new and dangerous thing.

When Jesus packed his bags and left Nazareth, and headed off to Capernaum, he was starting something new and dangerous that continues to this day. As we go forward in this New Year, there are bound to be changes ahead—changes in our personal lives and in our life together as a Church. I pray we be open to those changes, and willing to leave our comfort zones, and to believe that God is at work in the changes, and that God is taking us to a new thing.

Fourth Sunday in Ordinary Time

First Reading: Zephaniah 2:3; 3:12–3
Responsorial Psalm: 146
Second Reading: 1 Corinthians 1:26–31
Gospel: Matthew 5:1–12a

We hear Jesus begin his most famous sermon today—known as the Sermon on the Mount. And at the very heart of that sermon is the part we've just heard: the part known as The Beatitudes.

Jesus singles out eight groups of people he calls "blessed":

The poor in spirit
Those who mourn
The meek
Those who hunger and thirst for righteousness
The merciful
The clean of heart
The peacemakers
Those persecuted for the sake of righteousness

These eight groups of people Jesus calls "blessed" make it sound like God has a preference for the poor, the weak, and the unfortunate. To believe that the poor, the sorrowing, the meek, and the persecuted are blessed seems absurd to many people.

Our secular culture has its own set of Beatitudes. They would sound something like this:

> Blessed are the rich and famous, for they shall have what they want.
>
> Blessed are the powerful, for their wills will be done.
>
> Blessed are the well-educated and successful for they shall own the earth.
>
> Blessed are the young and the beautiful for they shall be sought after and admired.

The values that our secular world trumpets are poles apart from the values and way of life Jesus presents in this Gospel today.

What are we to make of these Beatitudes?

Surely there's nothing virtuous or blessed about poverty and hunger and suffering! God doesn't want them, and God doesn't approve of them. And it's because he doesn't want those things that those who do suffer are so dear to him!

I think the key to understanding the Beatitudes of Jesus is to understand the first one. The rest simply develop some aspect of this first one.

Our translation today reads: "Blessed are the poor in spirit, for theirs is the kingdom of heaven." Another translation I like is a freer translation—given by the Scottish scripture scholar William Barclay. He offers an interpretive, expansive translation of the first Beatitude that, essentially, is: "Oh, the bliss of those who know their need for God!"

Who is Jesus talking about here? Well, above all, I think he's speaking about himself! In fact, the first part of all eight Beatitudes describe the sort of person Jesus is: poor in spirit, the sorrowing one, the merciful one, the peacemaker, the one who hungers and thirsts for holiness, and so on.

And the key Beatitude is that first one, in the translation by Barclay: "Oh, the bliss of those who know their need for God." This is what being "poor in spirit" means! It means knowing your need for God and your absolute dependence on God. It means realizing I'm not the self-sufficient person I like to believe I am!

And I think that people who feel the pinch of poverty, people who are sorrowing or being persecuted—they're normally better at this. They're better at knowing their need for God than the rich are!

There's a line from an old prayer (sometimes attributed to a 1916 hymn by Hugh Thomas Kerr entitled "God of Our Life, Through All the Circling Years") that says: "When we're strong, Lord, leave us not alone." That may sound a little odd to us. We might expect the prayer to say: "When we're weak, Lord, leave us not alone." And that would be a good prayer, too! But it's not this prayer.

The author of this prayer takes it for granted that when we're weak we recognize our need for God. It's when we feel strong that we're apt to forget God. When the cash is flowing in, and when our stomachs are full, and our hearts warm with the approval of others, we're apt to be too self-satisfied and so we can easily tune-out on God. And so, this prayer is saying: "When we're strong, God, pester us. Don't leave us in our smugness."

Or as the first beatitude puts it: Blessed are those who know their need for God...the kingdom of heaven is theirs!

FIFTH SUNDAY IN ORDINARY TIME

First Reading: Isaiah 58:7–10
Responsorial Psalm: 112
Second Reading: 1 Corinthians 2:1–5
Gospel: Matthew 5:13–16

❧

In the chapter of Isaiah from which our first reading was taken today, we hear God's people ask: "Why should we fast if you never see it? Why do we do penance if you never notice?" God's silence is profoundly disturbing.

Why doesn't God come when we call? Why doesn't God reward our devotion? Earlier in today's chapter from Isaiah, God says to the prophet: "Announce to my people their sins. Day after day they seek me as if they were a nation that acted uprightly and not forsaken its God" (Isaiah 58:1–2, NRSV).

That's the way God answered the chosen people when they wanted to know where he had gone.

It is not I who have forsaken you, God says to the people, but you who have forsaken me. If you can't hear me, it's because you have strayed far from my voice.

The big disillusionment for the chosen people was that God was not where they thought! They thought God was supposed to be with them when they prayed, and fasted, and studied their scriptures. They thought nothing pleased God more than to find them on their knees, dressed in sackcloth and covered with ashes. But they were wrong! "This is the fast I want," God says to the sackcloth and ashes crowd.

The big disillusionment for the chosen people was that they couldn't serve God without serving their neighbors! Their relationship to God was not separable from their relationship to other people—especially the least of them! They had hoped they could keep their faith a private matter between them and their God, but that turned out to be an illusion.

Authentic religion can never be a private matter. It can never be something just between me and God!

And this is what Jesus is getting at in the Gospel today. He knows we may be tempted to hide our faith—to keep it very private—to keep it under the table, so to speak. And so, he gives us those images of salt and light, and says to us: "You have to be light for others; you have to be salt for others."

My Christianity is not just for me! It's for the sake of others, also. And if it's not for the sake of others too, it goes flat.

So, we can be sure God is going to try to break down the illusion we often have of being separate from one another. And that, therefore, we don't need to become involved with one another. We can't hide ourselves from other people—especially needy people—without hiding ourselves from God!

What God wants of us is to surrender our illusion of separateness. We have to figure out how to pool our resources so that the hungry can have bread, and the homeless can have shelter.

If God is silent, it may be because we're not speaking God's language yet. But there's a solution to that. God has taught us how to break the silence, and God has even given us the words!

"Here I am," God says in the reading from the prophet Isaiah

Fifth Sunday in Ordinary Time

today. These are the words we long to hear from God. But they're also the words God longs to hear from us. God longs for us to stand before a needy friend or neighbor, and say: "Here I am!"

We can be absolutely sure of this: Christianity can NEVER be private or uninvolved.

SIXTH SUNDAY IN ORDINARY TIME

First Reading: Sirach 15:15–20
Responsorial Psalm: 119
Second Reading: 1 Corinthians 2:6–10
Gospel: Matthew 5:17–37

Rabbi Jesus continues preaching his most famous sermon this evening—the sermon known as the "Sermon on the Mount." We heard the beginning of that sermon two Sundays ago—when the Gospel gave us the famous "Beatitudes"—beginning: "Blessed are the poor in spirit, for theirs is the kingdom of heaven."

In today's Gospel, Jesus is saying things about religious observance the crowd has never heard before. And it angered them! In fact, Jesus is digging his own grave whenever he speaks as he does here. He would never have been murdered had he chosen to speak only on nonchallenging, noncontroversial matters. But no. He had to go on and afflict the comfortable. "Don't suppose I've come to bring peace to the earth," he once said. "I've come not to bring peace, but a sword" (Matthew 10:34).

The sword he brings in this section of Matthew today is a challenge to the way most people understood their Jewish religion.

In effect, what Jesus is saying here and in other parts of the Gospel, might be put this way: "You have been placing the wrong emphasis on religion. What you think is most important is loyalty to the law rather than loyalty to GOD, the law-GIVER!" And this has to change. I've always liked what C. S. Lewis once wrote (in *Letters to an American Lady*):

> No one can make the Christian life into a strict system of law for two reasons: First, it raises scruples when we don't keep the routine. And secondly, it raises presumption when we do. Nothing gives one a false conscience more than keeping the rules—even if there has been a total absence of all real charity and faith.

As the Sunday Gospels unfold during the year, Jesus will persist in giving a new focus to Judaism. We will hear him say often, and in different ways: Listen to ME! Observe ME! Follow ME!

He doesn't attempt to set down a detailed code of conduct for us. Instead, he simply says: "I am the Way." Walk with ME. Learn from ME! Take on MY heart, MY desires.

I think this is what Jesus is getting at in this Gospel tonight when he tells his disciples: "Unless your holiness surpasses that of the scribes and Pharisees, you will not enter the kingdom of heaven."

Here Jesus is pointing to a more developed standard of morality than what previous generations of Jewish rabbis had proposed. He quotes three of the ten commandments—those on murder, adultery, and false oaths—and then gives his own teaching on them.

Each time he begins with the formula: "You have heard that it was said,..." And then he follows this by: "But I say to you..." Each time it's an invitation to go deeper than the teaching God gave to Moses on Mount Sinai.

Each time he's saying, in effect: "God taught you through Moses, but now I'm teaching you something MORE!"

No one had ever spoken like this before! And it's difficult for us to realize just how shocking it was for the people listening to him.

Jesus is assuming the role of a new Moses here! A new lawgiver for God's people! And his intent was not to break with Judaism, but

105

to bring Judaism to its fulfillment. He wants his followers to become the most exemplary Jews the world had ever seen!

His concern here in this Gospel today is not just with the sinful actions of murder, adultery, and false oaths but with what causes them to happen. Murder begins in an angry heart, just as adultery begins in a lustful heart, and false oaths begin in a deceitful heart. All the great Christian writers through the centuries have sent the message: "Look inward, and pay attention to the desires and attitudes that are forming in your heart." And why is this so important to do? Well, I think it's because it gives us the best, and most reliable, gauge of our spiritual and moral health!

Lent begins this year in just ten days. And on the first day of Lent, in the very first Scripture reading, we will hear God say through the prophet Joel: "Return to me with all your heart. Let your hearts be broken, not your garments torn" (Joel 2:12–13).

And at the very end of Lent, we hear God again, through the prophet Ezekiel: "I will cleanse you and give you a new heart, and put within you a new spirit. I will take out of your body the heart of stone and I will give you a heart of flesh" (Ezekiel 36:25–26, NJB).

This is what our Gospel is getting us ready for today!

SEVENTH SUNDAY IN ORDINARY TIME

First Reading: Leviticus 19:1–2, 17–18
Responsorial Psalm: 103
Second Reading: 1 Corinthians 3:16–23
Gospel: Matthew 5:38–48

❧

It's hard to believe, but Lent is around the corner! It doesn't seem all that long ago that we were celebrating Christmas and New Year's. But here we are! And for the next five and a half weeks, the Scripture readings and prayers of the Mass will be inviting us to consider where we are with the Lord, and how things are going between us. Any personal relationship deserves this kind of attention from time to time. Otherwise, it will surely deteriorate.

In the readings today we get a preview of Lent. It comes with the opening lines from the Old Testament reading: "Be holy for I, the Lord, your God, am holy."

And, in the last verse of the Gospel reading, we hear Jesus say: "So be perfect, as your heavenly father is perfect."

These words: "Be holy" and "be perfect" are very intimidating, aren't they? They seem so impossible to fulfill! And the people who think they are holy and perfect are pretty hard to take. I remember St. Theresa of Avila writing that people who were saints in their own eyes caused her more fear than all the sinners she ever met!

107

The New Jerusalem Bible translation of the Gospel words of Jesus about being perfect is this: "You must set no bounds to your love, just as your heavenly Father sets no bounds to his love." Now that, to me, clears up a lot of difficulty with the translation we have in our Gospel today: "Be perfect, as your heavenly Father is perfect." For being perfect is really about being more loving—and wanting to do more than I'm currently doing. Lovers understand this. Lovers know that love can't possibly be content with staying always the same! True love is always thinking about what more it can do.

Do you recall the incident in the Gospel when a young man comes up to Jesus and tells him: "I've kept all the commandments, now what more can I do?" And do you remember how our Lord reacted to him? Mark's Gospel says Jesus looked at him and loved him! (see Mark 10:17–21).

Jesus was thrilled to hear him ask: "Is there something more I can do?" It would be very disheartening for him if the question had been: "How little must I do?" "What's the minimum I must do in order to be Christian?"

In the Gospel today—and last Sunday too—Jesus is teaching about THE MORE. In essence he says: "You've been taught an eye for an eye. And you've been taught to hate your enemies. Well, I'm going to teach you something better!"

By the way, that Old Testament teaching: "an eye for an eye" is very sound moral teaching! I only wish it were better observed in the world than it is. The meaning of it is—ONLY an eye for an eye. Nothing more than that! It seeks to prevent disproportionate retaliation for injuries received. And there's so much of that in the world today! People acting out their revenge with little or no control. And not just violent acts, but more civilized acts of revenge like lawsuits. I might not pick up a club and beat you, but I'll take you to court and sue you for as much as I can get!

Revenge is a dark and dangerous thing—coming from an angry, malicious heart.

Jesus comes along and says that much better than an "eye for an eye," much better than controlled and measured retaliation, is no retaliation at all! Don't try to get even.

Instead, love your enemy.

Now this is about as high a moral standard as you can get, isn't it? And remember, love is in the will. It's a decision—to treat you as I would want you to treat me. With this moral standard, I'm being asked to love people I don't like, and people who don't like me, and who behave toward me in ways that are altogether unlovable. I'm being asked that no matter what a person does to me, or how a person treats me, I will not seek revenge. I will not wish harm to the person who has wronged me.

"Be holy as the Lord, your God, is holy." This is God's word to us this morning. What makes us holy, what makes us most like God, and what makes us fully human, is the sort of love that never gives up on people—no matter what people do to it.

EIGHTH SUNDAY IN ORDINARY TIME

First Reading: Isaiah 49:14–15
Responsorial Psalm: 62
Second Reading: 1 Corinthians 4:1–5
Gospel: Matthew 6:24–34

"The Lord has forsaken me. My Lord has forgotten me." Words from the prophet Isaiah in our first reading tonight. I'm sure you've heard these words spoken before. Probably you've spoken them yourself more than once. The feeling of utter aloneness and desolation is a dreadful feeling to have. Especially when you feel abandoned by God!

Yet in that same first reading tonight, Isaiah is quick to give what is perhaps the most consoling image of God in the whole of the Hebrew Bible—the tender image of God as a nursing mother. We know that a nursing mother cannot forget her child for more than a few hours. After a few hours, her own body reminds her that there's a child waiting to be fed. Her breasts begin to ache from fullness, and so she can't help but remember her child's hunger. But even if she could forget, says Isaiah, God will never forget you!

With this powerful image, God is telling us that his heart is so filled with love that his fullness is a continual reminder to him of our poverty!

In this sense, we might even say that God needs us! Not because He lacks anything in Himself, but because his fullness is so pressing that it hurts God not to be able to give. This is a strikingly powerful self-revelation from God, and we need to hear it again and again because our tendency is not to believe it. The omnipotent God needs my love? Come on, you can't be serious!

In the Gospel today, Jesus preaches this same message in powerful imagery of his own. For most of us here tonight, the question: "What will I eat?" or "What will I wear?" are questions about the choices we make when we go to the supermarket, or to the closet where we keep our clothes. But the people listening to Jesus that day had real survival worries!

We here today are blest in this regard. We know where our next meal is coming from. But survival worries for us have been replaced by longer-term anxieties. Can I keep my job in the current economy? Will I be able to pay for my children's college education? Can I save enough for retirement? Will I stay healthy and be able to work? What if serious illness strikes me?

The message Jesus gives in this Gospel is infuriatingly simple: "Do not worry," he says. Perhaps you noticed that he repeats these same words three times in this brief Gospel. Because God cares for me and relates to me as a nursing mother to her child, and because God knows what I really need, God will provide! So, the worry over what will become of me is useless. The future lies as far outside my control as does my height or my life span!

What's infuriating about the advice not to worry is that I hate to be reminded of how little control I really have. I prefer to regard the future as a territory I can plan out, when in fact it's a wide-open space where anything can happen.

It all comes down to a question of trust. Where do I place my ultimate trust? In God? Or in what this Gospel calls "mammon"— the Aramaic word for money. For Jesus, God and money are both competing for my worship and my trust.

The kind of worry and anxiety that can cripple us comes from putting our trust in what is ultimately not trustworthy, something we know may let us down. Far too many people in the post Enron, post Bernard Madoff years have learned this the hard way.

So, for all of us, worry is a deeply spiritual problem. It's a sign of our lack of trust in a good and loving God who cares for the "lilies of the field" and "the birds of the air." And aren't we worth more than they?

There's a prayer that's said at Mass just after the Our Father that begins: "Deliver us, Lord, from every evil and grant us peace in our day. In your mercy, free us from sin and protect us from all anxiety..." Please notice that the prayer links sin and anxiety together as forms of real evil from which we pray to be free.

People usually realize when they've sinned and the harm this causes to themselves and others. What amazes me is that people can be worried and anxious for years and years and never realize the harm they're doing to themselves. As a matter of fact, etymologists tell us that the word *worry* comes from an Old English word meaning "to seize by the throat and strangle." That pretty much sums up the suffocating effect that worry can have on us, doesn't it?

Sometimes you may wonder: Where am I with God? Am I growing spiritually? What may God be asking of me? Am I becoming the person God wants me to be?

In the light of the two major Scripture readings today, I think another way of putting the question is this:

Am I worrying less about the future?

Am I becoming more comfortable leaving the unknown future in the hands of God?

Am I willing to trust more the loving God of the Scripture readings today who is more concerned for me than a nursing mother for her child?

NINTH SUNDAY IN ORDINARY TIME

First Reading: Deuteronomy 11:18, 26–28, 32
Responsorial Psalm: 31
Second Reading: Romans 3:21–25, 28
Gospel: Matthew 7:21–27

❧

—Not included in this collection—

TENTH SUNDAY IN ORDINARY TIME

First Reading: Hosea 6:3–6
Responsorial Psalm: 50
Second Reading: Romans 4:18–25
Gospel: Matthew 9:9–13

"In their affliction, people will say: 'Let us strive to know the Lord. As certain as the dawn is his coming…He will come to us like spring rain that waters the earth.'" This is how our first reading begins today—a Reading from the Old Testament prophet, Hosea. "Let us strive to know the Lord."

A few weeks ago, I was on 125th Street, walking toward the Lexington Avenue subway, when someone handed me what I thought was an advertisement for a new cellular phone service or for a new clairvoyant in the neighborhood who could claim to see into your future. I'm sure you've been handed fliers like these. To my surprise, this was a flier from a Pentecostal church in the neighborhood. It began: "The most important thing in the world is to know God. It is a life-and-death matter." Wow, I thought. They sure have that right!

I thought back to that leaflet when I read this message from Hosea today, and the message of Paul in our second reading. If the most important thing in life is to know God, then the second most important thing in life, I think, is to have faith in God and faith in God's promises.

Faith is what Paul is passionate about in his letter to the Christian community in Rome—written in about the year AD 58. We'll be hearing sections from that letter every Sunday, beginning today and through the summer, until September.

Paul wants his readers to know that we all need the saving power of God, and that God has revealed his salvation in a new way that's quite apart from the way they had thought. They had always thought that the way we come to God—the way to salvation—was by careful observance of all the rules and commandments found in the first five books of the Bible. This was the Jewish way to live so as to be right with God. But Paul has a completely new teaching for them. We come to God, says Paul, not through what we can do ourselves, but through faith in what God has done for us. That was revolutionary for the Jewish people.

Paul points to the example of Abraham and Sarah, the ancestors of the Hebrews. Their story is told in the very beginning of the Bible, in the Book of Genesis. Abraham lived in the time before there were any prophets or scriptures or commandments from God to live by. God revealed himself to him. God inspired him. He must have been a very holy man. And God made promises to Abraham throughout his life. And Abraham was saved by his faith, Paul says. He believed what God had promised him at the beginning—that he and his wife Sarah would have descendants—despite the fact that both of them were very old. At that point in their lives, a child seemed impossible, but Abraham's faith in that promise never wavered.

So, Abraham and Sarah pulled up roots where they had been living—in the part of the world that is modern day Turkey—and began a journey of about 500 miles, not knowing where they were going, or where the journey would end! But they believed in God's promise to them. And they were convinced God would be faithful to his promise and would go with them and give them descendants.

Abraham and Sarah are the very first people in the Bible to live by faith. St. Augustine gives what may be the best description of faith when he says that "to have faith is to believe what you cannot see, and the reward of faith is to see what you believe."

To believe what you cannot see. How is that possible? How is it possible to believe what you cannot see? Paul sees us humans as being utterly incapable of doing what we ought to be doing. And to Paul's way of thinking, it's impossible to think that Abraham was a good man of strong faith, and so he was rewarded because he had such a strong faith. Paul wants to say that Abraham's faith was extraordinary precisely because he could never have developed it on his own! It was God's grace that allowed Abraham to have such amazing faith—even in the face of what seemed hopeless. The encounters Abraham had with God convinced him that God was a God who gives life to the dead and calls into existence things that don't exist. And for Paul, an encounter with the risen Christ works the same way. But what's absolutely critical is that encounter.

Do we really want an encounter with God? When we make space for that to happen, we find ourselves bereft of the things we normally put our faith in. Worldly power and influence, wealth, my own need to control things and to have clearly defined answers. If we're willing to let those go, we begin to get out of our own way and let God's grace do its work.

We can come to faith—faith in God and in God's promises. And this becomes our strongest security, our rock. And that faith will allow us to look the truly hopeless situation in the face and see hope. It will allow us to look at a casket being lowered into the ground and see not death, but a new and different life—to see not just an end but also a beginning. There's no way in the world we can believe this on our own. So, yes, as Hosea and Paul would agree: the most important thing in the world is to know God. And the second most important thing is to have faith in that God and in his promises.

Eleventh Sunday in Ordinary Time

First Reading: Exodus 19:2–6a
Responsorial Psalm: 100
Second Reading: Romans 5:6–11
Gospel: Matthew 9:36—10:8

❧

In Matthew's Gospel today, Jesus gives the twelve apostles their first missionary assignment. "Go to the lost sheep of Israel," he tells them, "and proclaim that the kingdom of heaven is at hand. Cure the sick, raise the dead, cleanse lepers, and drive out demons." This brings up the whole issue of miracles and the expectations we sometimes have of God in this regard.

Not too long ago I was in a hospital visiting a patient, and a woman met me at the elevator on my way out. She was quite upset. "Father," she said, "do you believe in miracles?" She went on to say she had just come from her sister's sick bed and that the doctors had told here there was no hope. I remember we were on the eighth floor and the elevator was on its way down. A priest's nightmare! What could I say in eight floors of an elevator ride?

I can't remember just what I did say, beyond trying to comfort her a bit and promising some prayers. It wasn't the time nor the place, but I wanted to say that I wasn't optimistic about the kind of miracle she was asking me about—when the doctors have given up all hope.

This is the extraordinary kind of miracle we find happening in the early days of the Church as a powerful help to the spread of faith in Jesus.

But such miracles are not common today. And the Church is very slow to claim that an authentic miracle has taken place in a given case. Even Jesus himself works relatively few miracles in the Gospels. He didn't heal all the sick. Not even most of them! And for a very good reason! Jesus didn't want to get the reputation, or to give the impression, of being a wonder-worker—a kind of magician who could bring a quick fix to a long-standing problem.

Who Jesus is, and what Jesus does, has little to do with being a wonder-worker or a psychic healer. He didn't want to attract people to himself who were primarily interested in the sensational and spectacular. And so, he frequently tells the people he's cured to be quiet about it! He knew that if you regarded him primarily as a miracle-worker you would miss the real meaning and purpose of his life. The physical cures he worked were always meant to be signs, pointing to something deeper. What any Gospel miracle is hinting at is that God's power resides fully in Jesus, and that this power is stronger than any evil. It reaches down into the most feared areas of human life, and it testifies that God is there, sharing the fear and the pain with us.

You notice today that the Gospel reading begins. "At the sight of the crowds, the heart of Jesus was moved with pity for them."

Scripture scholars will tell you that "pity" is not the best translation for the original Greek word here. The original Greek word is much stronger than our English word, *pity*. It comes from a word that means bowels! That's where the feelings of Jesus come from as he sees the troubled crowds. They come from deep down in his gut! And so better than *pity* is the word *compassion*. It is deep compassion that leads Jesus to cure the sick and resuscitate the dead.

But it's important to remember that the sick took sick again, and they died! And the dead who were raised, died again! The miracles were only hints of something that will be accomplished only in a new creation that won't be subject to disease or death. St. John writes about that in the Book of Revelation. "God will wipe every tear from your eyes. And there will be no more death, or mourning, crying out or pain. For the former world has passed" (21:4).

At the very end of the Creed we profess every Sunday, we say: "I look forward to the resurrection of the dead and the life of the world to come." That's what any miracle is pointing to. Any miracle is only a help to faith in that future reality where there will be no more mourning, or crying out, or pain.

And so, to that question at the hospital elevator: Do I believe in a God of miracles? A God who will intervene when doctors have given up all hope? Yes, I believe God can intervene in that way. But at the same time, I have to face the fact that God usually doesn't! Would I pray for a cure when death seems inevitable? Yes, I probably would. But there would be a second part to my prayer, a very important second part. Because I would pray that if the miracle didn't happen, I would have the strength to accept the outcome. And not just to accept it, but to be at peace with it. And I think that's the really important part of any prayer for a miracle!

TWELFTH SUNDAY IN ORDINARY TIME

First Reading: Jeremiah 20:10–13
Responsorial Psalm: 69
Second Reading: Romans 5:12–15
Gospel: Matthew 10:26–33

We all have our favorite Scripture passages, I'm sure. And we have our favorite images from the Bible, as well. One of my favorite images comes up today in this Gospel: the image of a single sparrow falling out of the sky and dropping to the ground. That doesn't happen, Jesus says, without God knowing about it!

"So, there's no reason to be afraid of anything," Jesus tells his disciples, "for you are worth more than many sparrows."

In this brief Gospel passage this morning, Jesus repeats that bidding three times! "Do not be afraid." I hope you know that these words of Jesus are among his most repeated words to us in the Gospels!

I'd like to say something about fear and worry and anxiety this morning.

I think we all sense high anxiety throughout the nation as the new government in Washington struggles to find its footing, and as terrorist attacks increase around the world.

Seventy years ago, the English-American poet W.H. Auden

published a long dramatic poem meant to frame modern man's condition. He entitled the poem: "The Age of Anxiety." Just two weeks ago, *The New York Times* referred to Auden's famous work, and claimed that we've entered a NEW Age of Anxiety! ("Prozac Nation Is Now the United State of Xanax," Alex Williams, June 10, 2017). To quote the article: "We've been at war for 14 years and have seen 2 recessions....Work life has changed. Everything we consider to be normal has changed. And nobody seems to trust the people in charge to tell them where they fit into the future!"

In our religious tradition, the Bible is filled with stories about worried and anxious people. Most people I know worry about all kinds of things.

Adolescents worry about their bodies and how they look, and whether they're acceptable to their friends. Parents worry about their children. Will they make the right friends? Will they do the right things and avoid the wrong things? Will they grow up to be good and caring people?

Adult children worry about aging parents. The elderly become anxious and worried over what will happen to them at the end of their lives. How will they wind up?

Many of our fears are related to the fear of LOSS. We worry about losing our health, and losing our independence. We fear losing our jobs, and our financial security.

Most of all we fear the loss of life. We fear death! We fear the death of those close to us, and we fear our own death.

So, it's not surprising to me that one of the most frequent words of God to us in the Bible is the very simple one we hear today. "Don't be afraid." Jesus is not saying: "Don't be afraid because nothing bad is ever going to happen to you." He knew better. He knew some things in life will go well and some will not. Some things will happen the way we envision them happening, and some will not.

Most of life is beyond our control. And in our better moments, we can be grateful for that. Because it's far better that the future be under God's control, than under my control! If I'm spending a lot of time worrying and being anxious about the future, I really don't trust in God's providential care for my life. At times like that we have to remind ourselves of the wisdom behind the adage that says: "I don't know what the future will bring, but I know who brings the future!"

Yes, God brings the future. But what's more wonderful still: God is in the future! For that reason, we don't need to know the details of the future. We don't need to get tied up in knots with anxiety about how it will all turn out.

Please know that worry and anxiety can never be pleasing to God! And never comes from God. On the contrary, it's a favorite tactic of the evil spirit—who seeks to send us into turmoil, and rob us of peace.

Worry can be a slow suicide. It can be a killer. In fact, etymologists tell us that the word *worry* comes from an Old English word meaning "to seize by the throat and strangle!" That's what worry does. And it's evil. Jesus invites us in the Gospel today to let go of our fears. And his constant message—throughout the Gospels—is: "Don't be afraid. You may not know what tomorrow will bring. But I will bring tomorrow. And I will be in the tomorrow. There's no reason to fear tomorrow! Because I am already there."

That's one of the basic messages of the New Testament. And I hope you are able to hear and believe it this morning.

THIRTEENTH SUNDAY IN ORDINARY TIME

First Reading: 2 Kings 4:8–11, 14–16a
Responsorial Psalm: 89
Second Reading: Romans 6:3–4, 8–11
Gospel: Matthew 10:37–42

✒

A few weeks ago, I was talking to one of our parishioners. Grace
is not her real name, but I don't want to give her real name. "I'm
afraid to die," Grace told me. Grace has had some serious health
problems, and besides, she's at an age when it's not unusual for
people to die! So, I wasn't surprised to hear her speak about death.
But what do you say when someone tells you they're afraid to die?

I thought of Grace when I read our second reading for today,
Paul's words to the Romans about death and new life. Paul teaches
that death has no power over us because Jesus survived death and
has promised that we also will survive death. This is one of the core
beliefs of our Christian faith. We can't get more basic than belief in
life after death, and in the resurrection of the body. It's part of the
Creed we say together every Sunday. And yet, it's not something we
often think about. Unless we're in Grace's shoes. Or unless we're
grieving over the recent death of a loved one.

I think our most spontaneous response to illness and death is to try to prevent them! We try to avoid them. Or deny them. Or ignore them. Because they don't fit into our program for living!

If we get sick, our primary concern is to get better as quickly as possible. If that doesn't happen, then we try to persuade ourselves—and those closest to us—that it may not be as bad as it looks and that everything will be all right again. And if death does come, we're often surprised, deeply disappointed, or even angry.

One of the great human beings of modern times was Dr. Elizabeth Kubler-Ross. She became famous for her work with the terminally ill. She wrote her landmark book in 1969 titled "On Death and Dying: What the Dying Have to Teach Doctors, Nurses, Clergy and Their Own Family." It's never been out of print! She outlines five stages that many terminally ill people go through in confronting their deaths. Here they are: Stage One: Denial. Stage Two: Anger. Stage Three: Bargaining. Stage Four: Depression. And the Final Stage: Acceptance.

Not all dying patients follow the same progression, she says, but most people experience two or more stages. Dr. Kubler-Ross was born into a Christian family and was a firm believer in life after death. "Why should death be horrifying?" she once posited to an interviewer. She continued, "Life doesn't end when you die….You'll just be somewhere else!"

That was her firm belief. But I think for many people, terminal illness and death are still the chief enemies of life.

In my experience many sick people die without ever giving much thought to their death, and without talking about it with their loved ones. And so, families are left unprepared. I'm thinking of someone who recently died, and where it was obvious he didn't have long to live. But even so, it was very difficult to prepare him properly for death.

He was surrounded with tubes and machines and busy nurses, that one got the impression he had to be kept alive at any cost!

This is a pitiful situation. Kubler-Ross used to say she believed death can be one of the greatest experiences ever! And that if we live each day of our life right, then we have nothing to fear! "You've got to approach your dying the way you live your life," she once said, "with curiosity, with hope, with fascination, with courage, and with the help of your friends."

I'm convinced we don't think enough about life after death. The New Testament is filled with the promise of afterlife, but it doesn't give much description of what it might be like. We can only guess what such a life might be like, and all our guesses will be woefully inadequate. Because we can't imagine life that's beyond time and space. Yes, it's true, sometimes we have moments in this life when time seems to stop. It happens sometimes with an intense experience of human love.

Or at times when we're absorbed in music, or in a work of art, or in the appreciation of nature: the beauty of a flower, or a starry night. We don't look at our watches at these times because we're not conscious of time. There is no "next" minute, or "next" hour. Because it's all NOW! It's all in the present that cannot become past! This is what eternal life must be like! No passing of time to bring an end to the present, intense experience of joy. In one of the final pages of the New Testament (in the Book of Revelation), we hear one of the great promises about life beyond death: "God will wipe away all tears from their eyes. There will be no more death, and no more mourning or sadness. The world of the past has gone" (Revelation 21:4, NJB).

We have to keep coming back to these promises and pray for a deeper trust that God is utterly faithful to his promises. Death is not the grim reaper some think it is! Death and dying is part of life! A normal process. The more we think about it, and talk about it—not in any maudlin way—the more comfortable we can become with it.

This is what I want to tell my friend Grace when I see her again. I think Grace may not have much time left on this earth. In the time left to her, I want her to know she has nothing to fear.

Fourteenth Sunday in
Ordinary Time

First Reading: Zechariah 9:9–10
Responsorial Psalm: 145
Second Reading: Romans 8:9, 11–13
Gospel: Matthew 11:25–30

＊

In the Gospel today Jesus says: "Come to me all you that are weary and are carrying heavy burdens, and I will give you rest" (NRSV).

This is one of the most consoling verses in all of Scripture! It's a passage you can find etched on tombstones, and worked into stained glass windows. How very comforting to hear Jesus invite us to turn to him when our burdens seem impossible to bear, or when our best efforts to cope with them have failed and we feel close to collapse! The promise he makes here is to lift the burden off our backs and replace it with a lighter yoke—lighter because it yokes us with one who is greater than we are, and whose strong help can enable us to bear any burden.

Some years ago, I came across a little story that helps, I think, to bring alive the promise Jesus makes in this Gospel today. I've used the story before, and you may have heard it. But I like it so much that I'll risk repeating it again today!

You could call the story a parable, I guess, like the parables Jesus tells in the Gospels. It clearly is the work of someone's imagination and doesn't pretend to be something that actually happened. I won't say anything about the story—just tell it to you and encourage you to think about it, and to draw your own conclusions.

The story goes this way. Once there was an older married couple who had raised several children and were now coming to retirement age. But they had little rest—because everywhere they went in the house and out and about, they carried several large bags of stones they had been collecting over the years. Some of the stones were large, some small. Some were natural stones right out of the soil around them, and some were pieces of brick or cement, made by human hands.

Every day the couple gathered stones from their children, from the neighbors, from each other, from the people at church, and from anyone who walked by their home that day. Their stones were worry rocks and bricks of fear, stones of hurtful memories, and rocks of unforgiving anger.

One day neighbors brought news that a young man had come to town to trade precious jewels for stones. The couple couldn't believe it! They thought it was some sort of trick. But they went to see him anyway, out of curiosity—and they carried their bags of stones with them.

The young man met them graciously and offered to exchange some of his precious jewels for their burdens. The woman was fearful and reluctant. But she handed over her heavy bag and was given a small bag of diamonds, a burden no heavier than a small purse. She felt thirty years younger! Light on her feet! And glad to be alive!

Her husband remained suspicious, though, and slowly took the stones, bricks, and rocks from his bag and began to trade and bargain for each one. The young man listened carefully to each account of fear and anger and hurt feelings, and then traded a small jewel for each heavy stone.

When it was over, the older man had a new and lighter burden to carry. And he went off feeling thirty years younger, and light on his feet, and glad to be alive!

And now comes the part of the story I like best:

As the young man watched the older couple walk away, he took each rock or stone they had left behind, and he smashed it. And from deep inside the stone, he drew forth a tiny precious jewel that he put into his bag—to save for the next person. In the heart of each heavy burden lay buried a jewel!

That's the brief parable I want to leave with you this morning. Like any parable, it's meant to get us thinking about the elements of the story. The message this little story brings is an unconventional one, and for some people, an absurd one. Namely, that in each of our heavy burdens lies buried a precious jewel!

We hear Jesus say in the Gospel today: "Come to me all you that are weary and are carrying heavy burdens, and I will give you rest" (NRSV).

And so, I'd like to pray this morning: "Lord Jesus, help us to discover the opportunities and the gifts that lie hidden in all our burdens."

FIFTEENTH SUNDAY IN ORDINARY TIME

First Reading: Isaiah 55:10–11
Responsorial Psalm: 65
Second Reading: Romans 8:18–23
Gospel: Matthew 13:1–23

⚜

J esus is teaching today from the prow of a boat because it's the only place he can find to sit. So many have come to hear him that there's no space left in their midst. So, he steps into a boat and speaks to them from across the water. If the crowds have come to him for teaching on practical pointers for their life, they're disappointed. What they get, instead, are more like dreams or poems. Jesus provides images of God's kingdom in descriptions as familiar as the crops in their own fields or the loaves of bread in their own kitchens, but with a new twist. Jesus seems to be saying that these ordinary things have something important to do with God's purpose for them.

The parables he tells them conceal his meaning. Some say this is how he stayed out of jail. He could have been arrested for preaching heresy and talking treason. But for talking about seeds and thorns, about good soil and bad? Not likely he'd be thrown into jail for that! By speaking in parables, Jesus could get his message across without saying it directly. His followers could nod in agreement while his critics could only scratch their bewildered heads! He speaks in parables, he says, so that only certain kinds of listeners can hear him—only listeners who are disposed to him and who have open minds.

Today's parable of the sower is a familiar one to most of us. A sower casts seeds on four different kinds of ground. First, the packed ground of a footpath, then ground that's full of rocks, then ground that's thick with thorns, and finally good fertile ground. Depending on where they land, the seeds are eaten by birds, or spring up quickly and then wither away, or get choked by thorns. But some of them— roughly a quarter of them—take root in good soil!

What this all means is carefully spelled out in the second half of the Gospel passage today.

The word of God is heard by many different kinds of people. It falls like seed into countless hearts, but it often fails to bear fruit. The fault is not in the seed but in the ground it falls on.

When we hear this story it's natural to wonder what kind of ground we are with regard to God. We start wondering how many rocks, and how many thorns, are in our field. And we wonder how we can turn ourselves into a well fertilized field to receive God's word. That's often the response we give to this parable. We hear it as a challenge to improve our life, so that God might find more fertile soil in us for the message God wants to sow.

We hear the story and think it's a story about ourselves. But what if it's not a story about us, but a story about the sower? What if it's not about our own successes and failures, but about the extravagance of a sower who isn't stopped by rocks and thorns? Who flings seed everywhere, wastes it lavishly, and just keeps on sowing— knowing the supply is inexhaustible.

If this is really the parable of the sower and not the parable of the different kinds of ground, then the focus is not on us and our shortcomings. Instead, the focus is on the generosity of our maker, the prolific sower who is not stopped by the condition of the fields, who is not stingy with the seed, but who casts it everywhere.

Fifteenth Sunday in Ordinary Time

Jesus grew up in an agricultural community, and the extravagance of nature, the abundance of seed that trees and plants produce year after year, spoke to him of his Father.

"The sower went out to sow." We can see him striding along, his purse bursting with seeds, the supply inexhaustible. He can afford to be lavish, scattering seeds all around him as he goes along. The Father is like this, Jesus is saying, scattering his love and his grace everywhere!

You know that one of the major questions that needs to get answered in everyone's lifetime is the question: Do you believe in God? You wouldn't be here today if you hadn't answered "yes" to that. But equally important is the question: what kind of God do you believe in? For some people, God is authoritarian and vengeful, an accountant in the sky who keeps a record of all our evil thoughts and actions. An angry father with a leather strap. That kind of God is not the one Jesus came to reveal. It's a story like this one today that's meant to show that. It's meant to show that God is extravagant beyond our understanding! That he's not calculating about the way he distributes his gifts. That he doesn't give only where he knows his gifts will be accepted. What concerns God is not quotas or effectiveness, but sheer abundance!

What best describes God is indiscriminate generosity! Now I ask you: Do you believe in that kind of God? A God who scatters his grace superabundantly and everywhere? For until that's your image of God, you have not understood the God that Jesus came to reveal.

SIXTEENTH SUNDAY IN ORDINARY TIME

First Reading: Wisdom 12:13, 16–19
Responsorial Psalm: 86
Second Reading: Romans 8:26–27
Gospel: Matthew 13:24–43

❧

Jesus loved to teach by telling stories that challenge us and get us thinking in new directions! The parable today about the wheat and the weeds in the farmer's field is profound, because it deals with one of the great mysteries of life—the mystery of evil. Often, we hear the mystery put in the form of a question. "If God is all good and all powerful, why does God allow so much evil and suffering in the world? Why suicide bombers and serial killers? Why corruption in government, in business and finance? Where does this come from? And why doesn't God intervene and do something about it?" We've all heard these questions, I'm sure. And we don't have answers for them.

In the parable today, Jesus sheds some small light on this huge mystery. What we learn from the parable is that God is not the source of evil in the world.

It comes from elsewhere—from what the parable calls the "enemy." What's more, God doesn't want it. We can never hold God responsible for the many evils that beset our world.

However, if God doesn't want evil, and if God is all-powerful, then why doesn't God get rid of it? We see that kind of thinking on the part of the servants in the story when they go to the owner of the field and ask him: "Do you want us to go out and pull the weeds up?"

But that wouldn't be as easy as it sounds. Matthew may make it sound like there are only two kinds of people in the world—the good and the bad, the wheat and the weeds. But that's too simplistic and unreal. Most of us can recognize that there's both wheat and weeds in ourselves, and in our neighbors, and in the world. Our fields are full of mixed plantings—not pure wheat, and not pure weed either.

The owner of the field, representing God in the parable, recognizes this conflict of opposites. And so, he isn't as troubled by the weeds as his servants are. "No. I don't want the weeds pulled out," he tells his servants. "Let them be. Let them grow together until the harvest."

Now if this is a story about evil in the world and about God's response to it, then what Jesus is saying is that God doesn't have any immediate plans to uproot the evil among us. God's plan, for now, is to wait—and let it be. And the reason he gives is that some of the good wheat might be destroyed if the weeds were uprooted. So, for the sake of the good wheat, they're left to grow together in a mixed field. At harvest time, the weeds will be discarded—but without injuring the wheat!

We learn something very important here. God is looking after the good of the wheat when God refuses to pull up the weeds. The good of the wheat is always God's first and overriding concern.

The first reading from the Book of Wisdom speaks of a God who "judges with clemency and with much lenience." Now could it be that a "lenient" God, a God who is "gracious and slow to anger" (from today's psalm), allows evil to remain in the world so as to give it time to be changed?

With enough time, diseases are often cured, and scars are healed. With enough time, enemies begin talking to one another.

Whenever people go about trying to change some of the evils in our world, something wonderful can happen. Sometimes the evil is corrected. Or if it isn't, sometimes we're the ones who change! We mature as human persons because we've faced up to the evils in our life. We haven't run away from them, or ignored them. Jesus hints at this in the story when he says that wheat can grow and come to maturity even when it's surrounded by weeds!

So, with this story today, God is asking us to tolerate a mixed field of wheat and weeds.

I want to leave you with a litany I discovered some years ago. It's a litany based on this Gospel parable today, and it goes like this:

> Wheat and weeds – Let them grow together.
> Arabs and Jews in the Middle East—Let them grow together.
> Documented and undocumented aliens—Let them grow together.
> Rich and poor, humble and mighty—Let them grow together
> Days of sparseness and days of plenty—Let them grow together
> Joys and sorrows, laughter and tears—Let them grow together
> Doubt and faith—Let them grow together
> Virtue and vice—Let them grow together.
> All contraries of the Lord—Let them grow together!

We're being asked to take the long-range view of things here!

Let me end with a quote from Pope Francis in an interview he gave to the editor of the Italian Jesuit periodical *La Civiltá Cattolica* this past September (Sept. 30, 2013):

> I have a dogmatic certainty: God is in every person's life.
> Even if the life of a person has been a disaster, even if it

is destroyed by vices, drugs or anything else—God is in this person's life. You must try to seek God in every human life. Although the life of a person is a land full of thorns and weeds, there is always a space in which the good seed can grow. You have to trust God.

SEVENTEENTH SUNDAY IN ORDINARY TIME

First Reading: 1 Kings 3:5, 7–12
Responsorial Psalm: 119
Second Reading: Romans 8:28–30
Gospel: Matthew 13:44–52

The first reading this morning began with God saying to King Solomon: "Ask something of me and I will give it to you." Isn't that amazing? What wonderful words for God to speak to anyone! Can you imagine God saying that to you? Do you think it would be unusual of God to want you to ask for something, and then to actually give you what you have asked for?

I don't think that's so unusual! And if you've ever had the experience of prayers being answered, you won't think it unusual, either! What was unusual, I think, was what Solomon asked for from God. He asked for an understanding heart—so that he could make right choices and right decisions.

He had found himself king at a very young age and knew he needed help.

What a world this would be if those who held power were persons whose main desire was to make the right decisions and have an understanding heart!

In the Gospel parables today, Jesus speaks about a person searching for a valuable pearl, or for a treasure buried in the ground. Both the Gospel and the first reading raise some questions for us this morning. I think we're being invited to reflect on what we consider to be the truly valuable things in life.

What are the things I most treasure?

What is the one really valuable pearl I would sell everything to own? God always meets us on the level of our deep desires. And the readings this morning are an invitation to you and me to be in touch with them.

I should be able to name my deepest desires if you were to ask me. And I should be able to name the deep desires of my heart to God—if God were to ask me, as God asks Solomon today.

This reminds me of the words from Jesus—in the Gospel of Mark—to a blind beggar who was persistent in seeking him out. "What do you want me to do for you?" Jesus asks him (Mark 10:51). These are thrilling words from Jesus—Jesus, rich in gifts—to a poor, blind beggar. I think it would be wonderful if you could imagine Jesus facing you and asking you that same question: "What do you want me to do for you?"

It matters a great deal to the Lord what our hearts deeply desire, and he really does want to see those desires fulfilled, not frustrated.

The desires of our heart have a way of changing, though, as we go through life. What I most desire at, say, age sixty is probably quite different from what I most desired at age forty, or at age twenty, or at fourteen. It was Rabbi Abraham Heschel who once said: "When I was young, what I most admired were clever people. Now that I am old, kind people are the people I most admire."

Our values and priorities shift. Hopefully in that process I come to discover what the truly valuable pearls are. And then to set my heart on them! I need to be able to say: "These are the things that really matter. Those other things don't."

But it usually takes time to come to that discovery. So often we spend a lot of time and energy pursuing things that in the long run are not really important at all.

It would be a good thing in the weeks and months ahead to take a close look at the things we've been seeking after and praying for. God says to Solomon today: "Because you have NOT asked for a long life, nor for riches, nor for the life of your enemies, but for an understanding heart, I give you what you requested."

So, this should lead us to wonder this morning: "Have I been asking God for the right things? Is my heart set on real pearls, or on fake ones?"

Eighteenth Sunday in Ordinary Time

First Reading: Isaiah 55:1–33
Responsorial Psalm: 145
Second Reading: Romans 8:35, 37–39
Gospel: Matthew 14:13–21

❧

—Not included in this collection—

NINETEENTH SUNDAY IN ORDINARY TIME

First Reading: 1 Kings 19:9a, 11–13a
Responsorial Psalm: 85
Second Reading: Romans 9:1–5
Gospel: Matthew 14:22–33

❧

Today's Gospel story of the apostles caught in a storm at sea has long been a favorite of mine. It seems like more than just a miracle story. It seems to be a parable of the human condition. You could say the story is about all of us! We are the ones "at sea"—an expression we use fairly often. We realize life's passage is not a smooth one. It's rudely interrupted by troubles of all sorts—family troubles, financial troubles, sickness, death. We often seem to be in a very small boat, tossed about on a stormy sea, with the wind and the waves not behind us, helping us along, but in front of us, causing havoc.

And Jesus is not with us in our boat! We're quite alone, and at the mercy of the storm. Not only is Jesus not with us, but he delays quite awhile before coming to the help of his friends. And by the time he does come to them—walking across the water—they're so terrified that they mistake him for a ghost. "Take courage," he tells them. "It's me! Don't be afraid."

We are so anxiety-prone that the Church has inserted a prayer at every single Mass, just after the Lord's Prayer, the Our Father—a prayer that reads: "Deliver us, Lord, from every evil. In your mercy keep us free from sin and protect us from all anxiety." Wherever a Mass is being said, we pray for our daily bread. And wherever a Mass is being said, we pray to be free from anxiety!

In the Gospel story, Peter is reassured when he hears Jesus say: "It's me. Don't be afraid." And so, he starts moving out of the boat onto the water—moving steadily toward Jesus—until he notices again how strong the winds and the waves are. And then Peter does a foolish thing—but an understandably all too human thing. He allows the storm that's raging outside and around him to come inside him, and to cause even greater fear and anxiety to return. Peter begins to sink in deep water because he's taken his eyes off Jesus and has become absorbed in the storm around him. The more he turns from Jesus, and the more he focuses his thoughts on the storm, the more he begins to drown.

This is a parable about the human condition. It's a story about all of us! In the hard times, it often seems we're drowning and God is nowhere around.

The is also a parable about faith. Jesus invites Peter to come to him. And so, Peter has to leave the security of his boat and step onto the water without any support. This is a wonderful image for faith. Because having faith is much like being at sea and having to face the risk of the unknown, but with a confidence that Jesus is with me, close by.

When Peter begins to sink, he cries out to the Lord to save him. And we notice that the Lord's response is not to calm the storm, but simply to be with Peter in the storm! He reaches out his hand to Peter and hauls him out of the turbulent waters like a big, frightened fish. And then the awful words: "O you of little faith. Why did you doubt?"

These are the same words many of us ask ourselves every day. Why don't I have more faith? Why can't I trust God? Why am I afraid to let go and let God care for me? Why do I doubt?

I believe in God. I believe God has my best interests at heart. But then I lose my job. And my savings begin to disappear. And my faith goes with them, and I begin to sink.

I believe in life after death, but then I get sick and the doctor says six, maybe nine months. I pray for a miracle, but no miracle comes. And I pray for the reassuring voice of God, but no voice comes. And the waves start to creep up my legs, and I begin to sink.

Why do we doubt? I think we doubt because we're afraid. Because the sea is so vast, and we are so small. Because the storm is so powerful, and we are so easily drowned. Because life is so beyond our control, and we feel so helpless in its grip. We doubt because we're afraid—even when we do have faith! It's not as though we had none. We have some! Like Peter, we have a little faith, and a little is better than nothing. Like Peter, we have faith, and we doubt. We try to walk with Jesus, and we fail. We take a few steps, and we begin to sink.

What if Peter had not sunk? What if he had jumped out of the boat with perfect confidence in the Lord and just glided over to Jesus without a moment's hesitation—while the storm and the winds were raging around him? Well, then it would be a different story! It might even be a better story, but it wouldn't be a story about us! The truth about us is more complicated. The truth about us is that we believe and we doubt. We walk, and we sink. It's not that we do only one or the other. We do both. Both our faith and our doubt exist in us at the same time. They lift us up, and they weigh us down. But that's the human condition! If we had no doubts, no fears—if we could walk on water all by ourselves—we would not need the Lord. We could save ourselves.

Our doubts and our fears may disturb us, but they remind us of who we are. They remind us of our imperfect humanity. And they remind us of who it is that needs to be present in our lives, who it is we have to keep our eyes fixed on, to keep us from drowning!

TWENTIETH SUNDAY IN ORDINARY TIME

First Reading: Isaiah 56:1, 6–7
Responsorial Psalm: 67
Second Reading: Romans 11:13–15, 29–32
Gospel: Matthew 15:21–28

❧

In about ten sentences, St. Matthew in this Gospel story today gives us a perfect little, short story—complete with a happy ending. It's the only story in the Gospels that takes place outside of Jewish territory—north of Galilee, in what is now Lebanon. The main character in the story is a Canaanite woman—not Jewish, but a descendant of the original settlers whom the Jews had displaced.

This Canaanite woman appears on the scene and cries out to Jesus for help. Matthew describes the reaction of Jesus with some of the most chilling words in the New Testament! Matthew writes: "Jesus did not say a word in answer to her." Imagine! A cry for help is met with stony silence. Jesus says nothing to her! He does nothing! And he offers this explanation. "I was sent only to the lost sheep of the house of Israel."

But the woman doesn't accept that explanation as final. Instead, she stops calling out to him from a distance, and she comes up close and kneels at his feet. "Lord, help me."

143

We don't know if there was sternness in his voice when he answered her: "It's not right to take the food of the children and throw it to the dogs." But something about him must have encouraged her rather than discouraged her, and she speaks again. She admits it's not right to take food from children to give to dogs. But both she and Jesus use a word for dog that in Greek means "household dogs," house pets. So, his answer to her is not as rude as it may seem.

Anyone who has ever lived in a house with dogs and children knows how attentively a dog watches for some scraps and crumbs that are sure to find their way to the floor. If the children of the household are well-fed, then no one can begrudge the scraps of food that are given to household pets waiting under the table!

This pagan woman knows that what she's asking for is not all that out of line. She acknowledges she's not part of God's chosen people. Nevertheless, she's making a claim! She's making a claim—as a member of the household—to be provided for out of God's abundance! The God of Israel doesn't exclude Gentiles from his care and protection. And that's why Jesus says: "Woman, great is your faith! Let it be done for you as you wish." She shows faith in him. And so, he gladly responds to her need.

This incident was important for the early Church in Matthew's time. The recorded contacts of Jesus with non-Jews in the Gospels are rare. His ministry was to his own, to the Jewish people. They were the people God had chosen, and so they were the ones who had the first right to hear the good news. But by the time of Matthew's Gospel—roughly forty years after the death and resurrection of Jesus—the Church had reached out to Gentile people, particularly through the ministry of St. Paul and his disciples. By the time Matthew wrote about this Canaanite woman, there had been a large Gentile church in Rome for many years. And the prophecy of Isaiah in our first reading today was being fulfilled. God is a God for all peoples, writes Isaiah. Not just for the Jewish people! And that's why the psalm response for today is so appropriate: "O God, let all the nations praise you!" The Christian God has wide open arms! They never close anyone out.

This is reflected in the Third Eucharistic Prayer of the Mass which I'll be using shortly. In the Third Eucharistic Prayer, the Church prays that "this sacrifice which has made our peace with you may advance the peace and salvation of all the world."

And then this prayer: "Father, hear the prayers of the family you have gathered here before you. In mercy and love unite all your children, wherever they may be."

The Christian God is open to the whole wide world—not just to some. And this Gentile woman appears in our Gospel today to illustrate that! Praised be this God who is bigger, and more inclusive, than we could ever imagine!

TWENTY-FIRST SUNDAY IN ORDINARY TIME

First Reading: Isaiah 22:19–23
Responsorial Psalm: 138
Second Reading: Romans 11:33–36
Gospel: Matthew 16:13–20

✁

This Gospel scene today occurs near the end of our Lord's life when his thoughts were often on his own death and on the survival of the small group of disciples he had gathered around him. Every now and then he quizzes them...to see how much they're taking in...to see how well they've understood him.

Here, today, he asks an entirely different kind of question. Not a question about anything he has said, but about who he IS. He wants to know who people think he is. They offer a list of speculations. But he's not really interested in what they've heard about him. He doesn't want someone else's answer. He wants THEIR answer, so he presses them to declare themselves. "But who do YOU say that I am?"

The question is all important, and it calls for an intensely personal response—from each of us!

I think at some time in our adult life we ought to be able to answer that question for ourselves. And, of course, the best answer is not just something handed on to us from our parents, or from our early years in Catholic school, or after-school religious education programs—knowledge we may automatically carry with us for the rest of our lives. This is what someone once called an "inherited Christianity," not an experience of OUR OWN. This is because faith never becomes real and vital until it becomes your faith... something very personal, something you OWN! And this is always formed through your own questioning. And soul-searching.

When Peter heard "Who do you say that I am?" he was bold enough to answer: "You are the Christ, the Son of the living God." Peter came to that understanding only after close personal contact with Jesus, over an extended time.

Jesus is immensely consoled by that answer, and, in one fell swoop, he pronounces Peter blest—the rock upon which he will build his Church and the keeper of the keys to the kingdom. With keys being a symbol of power and authority!

But no sooner does Peter receive his new authority than he begins to argue with Jesus about the passion and death that's going to happen to him in Jerusalem! "Get behind me, Satan," Jesus says to him in next week's Gospel. "You are an obstacle to me" (Matthew 16:23).

In six sentences Peter goes from being blest to being satanic! From being the rock on which the Church is built to being a stumbling block in Christ's way! And that's because Peter's understanding of who the Messiah was to be was all wrong. Jesus was not the Messiah that Peter and the Jewish people expected him to be.

So, we can be surprised that Peter was selected for the number one position among the twelve. The picture we get of him in the Gospels is not all that flattering. At different times, he's impulsive and bull-headed, fearful and cowardly! About all that might be said in Peter's favor is that every time he falls down, he gets back up again. He brushes himself off and gets going again. Perhaps his flaws actually made him a better role model for leaders in the Church—leaders THEN and leaders NOW! Because Peter came to realize he didn't know all the answers.

And that he had to learn.

His experience of being wrong, and of being weak and fearful, taught him to listen to voices wiser than his own and to trust in the Lord's willingness to forgive him.

Peter may not have had the flawless character and the intellectual depth you and I might look for if we were choosing the first pope. But someone like Peter can probably understand us better—we who find it easy and safe to repeat other people's answers—because we haven't thought enough about our own answers!

If Peter is the rock on which the Church is built, then there's hope for us all! Because he shows us that what counts is not being perfect, but the willingness to keep on trying...and the willingness to get up again after we fall.

TWENTY-SECOND SUNDAY IN ORDINARY TIME

First Reading: Jeremiah 20:7–9
Responsorial Psalm: 63
Second Reading: Romans 12:1–2
Gospel: Matthew 16:21–27

❧

As you listen to the Gospel today, you might think this was Good Friday or a Sunday in Lent, rather than a Sunday in late August! Jesus is talking about his own passion, death and resurrection for the first time in Matthew's Gospel.

And the very mention of suffering and death gets Peter upset. Peter, christened "the rock" in last Sunday's Gospel, suddenly becomes more like a pile of sand! He takes Jesus aside. "God forbid that any such thing ever happen to you!" he blurts out.

Does that sound familiar? How often have you said, or thought: Oh, God forbid that he suffer! God forbid that she die. God forbid that I get sick. God forbid such a thing!

The reaction of Jesus is swift. The Gospel says he turned to Peter and said: "You are a stumbling block to me! You are setting your mind not on divine things, but on human things!" (NRSV).

And then Jesus goes on to say something that can make you feel very uneasy. "Anyone who does not take up his cross and follow me cannot be my disciple."

I find these are hard and disturbing words! When I hear them, I'm reminded of a popular song Irving Berlin wrote years ago called "Say It Isn't So." I thought of that song when I read the words of Jesus this morning about self-denial and the cross. The cross? Me? Say It Isn't So!

You know, I sometimes think if we had the chance, most of us would probably want to rewrite the Gospel! The story of the birth of Jesus would remain. It's a charming beginning! The healing miracles of Jesus would stay, and much of his teaching would stay. But the Sermon on the Mount would have to go. And so would his words today about the cross. We'd be left with a collection of nice sayings, something like an updated Book of Proverbs, or Ben Franklin's Maxims.

It was C. S. Lewis who once wrote that what we'd really like from the Gospels would be a God whose main concern was that we live an enjoyable, comfortable life, and whose plan for the world was that at the end of each day everyone could say: "I've had a wonderful day today!" (see *The Problem of Pain*).

No, there's no place for the cross in the Gospel most of us would rewrite! Who wants to be sick? Who wants a problem child? Who wants to be saddled with a worrisome, anxious disposition, or with a wretched temper that makes you snap at your best friends? Nobody!

And Christians are not masochists! We aren't supposed to go around looking for ways to suffer! The history of Christianity has too many examples of masochism masquerading as spirituality! Just because something is harder to do doesn't mean that it's better to do.

When I was a young novice in the Jesuit seminary, for a while I used to think I was always supposed to choose the more difficult path because, surely, the more difficult path was the better one, the more commendable one! I learned later on that wasn't true, and that there's no value in the cross for its own sake. In itself, the cross is absurd! God is not in favor of suffering! God is not in favor of the suffering of anyone! God is in favor of relieving suffering!

Twenty-Second Sunday in Ordinary Time

The cross makes sense only if it leads to life! Only if it makes us more human! Only if it makes us better persons! And often enough that will happen. Often, it's the handicapped person who has the greatest empathy for the handicaps of others. Often, it's the recovering alcoholic who is the most sensitive to the difficulties and the power of addiction. Often, it's the one who has been through a divorce who knows best how to heal broken hearts.

In our religion, Calvary makes sense only because it leads to Easter! If it had not led to Easter, Calvary would have been one more terrible instance of how we maim and kill one another. And we wouldn't be here today! Because there would be no Christianity, and the world would be a much darker place.

So, we shouldn't be surprised when crosses come along. Illness, financial troubles, new kinds of temptation. It's exactly through such situations that we have the chance to become more human—more patient and more loving, more trusting and more courageous—than we ever dreamed of being before.

TWENTY-THIRD SUNDAY IN ORDINARY TIME

First Reading: Ezekiel 33:7–9
Responsorial Psalm: 95
Second Reading: Romans 13:8–10
Gospel: Matthew 18:15–20

Have you ever faced the dilemma of whether or not to offer correction to a friend or a relative whose behavior has been hurtful, whether hurtful to self or to another?

This harmful behavior is what Jesus is speaking about in the Gospel this morning when he says: "If your brother sins against you, go and tell him his fault…." What Jesus is speaking about here is a serious sin or behavior problem. The context in which we hear the Gospel today is in the context of that second brief reading from Paul's Letter to the Romans where we hear once again the central commandment of the New Testament: to love one another.

What Jesus is doing in the Gospel is simply spelling out one of the very practical demands of love. What love demands is that we look out for one another! And, at certain times, that may involve correction of another.

All kinds of strong resistance can rise up in us against that sort of thing. The thought can come: "It's hard enough for me to

152

lead my own life correctly. So, what right do I have to offer correction to someone else?"

"Isn't that playing God?"

"Shouldn't I mind my own business?"

"Won't we become alienated from one another?"

These fears are very real and very common.

There's a strong social pressure in our culture to define my world increasingly in private terms. Besides, no one enjoys confronting another person. Some families will go for years before addressing a problem in a family member!

In the face of those real fears, the Scripture message today is clear. There are times when I have to say to a family member, or a friend, or a coworker: "You're hurting me." OR "You're hurting yourself." OR "You're hurting others." The Gospel says if this doesn't work, I may need the help of one or two others.

A dramatic instance of this sometimes happens in the treatment of an alcoholic when the immediate family or close friends gather for what's termed "an intervention." Out of their great concern, they confront the person who has a serious drinking problem and try to make the person aware of the seriousness of the problem and of the hurt being done.

When something is clearly hurtful about a person's behavior, and I stand back and say nothing, and do nothing, is this love? It seems more like indifference to me! Or simply the unwillingness to get involved. It would be like watching a crime take place and not doing anything about it—not even reporting it!

Love means watching out for one another! And that means I'm not as independent as I might think I am. Or as I might like to be.

My religion is not just something between me and God. It's something between me and God and the wider circle of people around me. That's the only religion Jesus preaches!

Twenty-Fourth Sunday in Ordinary Time

First Reading: Sirach 27:30—28:7
Responsorial Psalm: 103
Second Reading: Romans 14:7–9
Gospel: Matthew 18:21–35

Some years ago, I came across an unusual ad in *The New York Times*. It was a personal message from one individual to another. I'll never forget it! The size of the ad alone astonished me! It was not a full-page ad, but it was one quarter of a full page. Now that's a lot of space for a personal message in a daily newspaper. The message was addressed to Edith G. from Phil K. And this is what it said—in large, bold print.

> Edith. I had no self of which to share. I had no self capable of input, capable of commitment. But now that self has been nurtured—arduously, consciously nurtured. It is strong enough now to give of, unselfishly. Healthy enough now, fearless in not holding back. Please forgive me. Reconsider. Help make a new us, better now than before.

And it was signed: Phil.

What a remarkable, magnanimous thing to do! To make a confession of your sins and a plea for forgiveness in the morning paper! I was very moved by that. And I sometimes wonder what happened when Edith opened her newspaper that morning and read Phil's message to her. I'd like to think that something supernatural happened to her! I'd like to think that a miracle happened, and that she did reconsider and forgive. I'd like to think that a new life started for both of them that morning through that very public act of forgiveness.

And why? The answer is given in the Gospel parable today. It's not a complicated answer. I am being asked to keep on forgiving because God has forgiven me so much, and over so long a time! It's that simple. And if we don't realize God has forgiven us much and often, then we're being very blind and naive, for sure.

You know in the prayer that Jesus taught us and which we pray at every Mass, the Lord's Prayer, there are several petitions. And all the petitions are passive: "Thy Kingdom come," "Thy Will Be Done," "Hallowed Be Thy Name," and so on. The only thing we say that we will do in that prayer is forgive trespasses. Isn't that revealing? Isn't that an indication of how central and important forgiveness should be in our lives? How it's at the very heart of the Gospel?

The psalm response for today is from Psalm 103. It's a verse that's repeated often in Scripture: "The Lord is kind and merciful, slow to anger, and rich in compassion." Merciful, slow to anger, and rich in compassion! This is God's nature! And this is the way God asks us to be with one another.

But we need a lot of help for that! And what we can't do on our own, God can do for us.

I'm reminded of the advice given by one of our Jesuit saints, Alphonsus Rodriguez of Majorca, about four hundred years ago. "I place my bitterness between God and myself," he wrote, "until God changes it into sweetness."

Carrying around anger, hanging on to grudges and being unwilling to forgive, is like carrying around a very heavy weight that will eventually wear me down. If I harbor anger, I can't think right. I can't talk right, eat right, or sleep right. I'm being controlled by the person who has offended me. I'm being controlled by my negative feelings toward that person. To be free, and to be myself again, with God's help, I have to make the conscious decision to forgive. Then the poison will begin to drain out of my system, and the peace I long for will gradually come over me. This is the only way I can be free.

Twenty-Fifth Sunday in Ordinary Time

First Reading: Isaiah 55:6–9
Responsorial Psalm: 145
Second Reading: Philippians 1:20c–24, 27a
Gospel: Matthew 20:1–16a

✣

I'd ask you, for the moment, to imagine yourself as one of the workers in this parable who has worked all day long in the heat of the sun, and has been paid the same salary as those who have worked for one hour.

Your reaction is: "It's not fair!" Equal pay for equal work is fair. Equal pay for UNequal work is not! And you complain about that to the man who hired you. You complain that he has put you on an equal footing with those others who haven't done nearly what you've done. And you resent that. And as long as you're stuck in your resentment, it blinds you to the goodness in this man.

He really cared about all those people standing around waiting! He returned again and again to extend the invitation. He knew they all needed a full day's pay, or they and their families wouldn't eat. But his goodness doesn't impress you as long as you feel cheated, and as long as you can't realize that his hiring of you was itself a gift. It was not something you could claim you deserved.

In this parable and others like it, Jesus challenges us to stretch our understanding of God beyond where it is. This is not something I'm inclined to do. Most of us want to hold on to the image of God we've grown up with and have become accustomed to.

If I think God should reward the good and punish the evil in this world, if I think everything should run smoothly for me because I'm living a morally decent life, then inevitably I'm going to be very disappointed. And it's hard to relate to a God who is a disappointment!

The God Jesus came to reveal is a God far beyond what I can expect, or imagine! And far beyond the categories and protective boundaries we set. The God Jesus reveals is a God of astonishing and unpredictable surprises!

"My thoughts are not your thoughts, nor are your ways my ways," God tells us in our First Reading this morning. God's way is to give favors to those who have done little or nothing to deserve them! And that includes each one of us here this morning! Do you think you've deserved all the blessings that have been part of your life?

I think this parable today is God's way of telling us: I really am a good God, you know; far more good than you give me credit for, and far more good than you can imagine! And this is really important good news for us this morning! It's kind of embarrassing when we discover ourselves complaining about God's goodness to others, isn't it?

And so, the most important thing I have to say to you this morning is that when you think of God, you have to think BIG, and remain open and flexible and curious! You have to be prepared for surprises...for delightful, joyful surprises! Because God is always doing something unpredictable!

Let me tell you a true story. I've altered some of the details. A man had three daughters. When his wife died, they were all he had.

One daughter lived far away. She loved her father, but she lived a very busy life. She ran her own business, and was a caring mother to four children. She never had much time to travel and do things with her father. But she kept in touch with him and did what she could.

The second and third daughters lived in the same city as their father. The second was a bit wild. She had married young and divorced young. She wasn't very responsible and couldn't hold a job for very long. She had time on her hands but didn't think to spend much time with her father.

The third daughter had a family of her own that had its share of difficulties, but she invited her father to come and live with her. He did, and HER family became HIS family. Father and daughter went places together and grew ever more close.

After a few years, the father died. In his will he acknowledged his third daughter's special care for him, but he divided his estate into three equal parts. Each of the daughters received an exact third.

SURPRISE!

And how do you feel about it? Are your sensibilities shocked and offended? Or can you feel awe and admiration at the astonishing, unpredictable love of a father for his daughters?

God is always more generous than we can imagine! Shame on us when we begrudge Him that generosity!

TWENTY-SIXTH SUNDAY IN ORDINARY TIME

First Reading: Ezekiel 18:25–28
Responsorial Psalm: 25
Second Reading: Philippians 2:1–11 or 2:1–5
Gospel: Matthew 21:28–32

If there had been an inquest into the death of Jesus, this parable he tells today might be submitted as one of the things that got him killed. According to Matthew, Jesus told it during the last week of his life in Jerusalem—after he had chased the buyers and sellers out of the temple. He went back into the temple to teach, and that's when the chief priests and elders cornered him. They wanted to know who had given him authority to do such things.

Instead of giving them a straight answer, he told them this little story about the two brothers. One commentator has called them "the yes and no" brothers. "Which one did the will of his father?" Jesus asks them. It was an easy answer for them—as it is for us. Actions speak louder than words. That's obvious. It was not what either son said that mattered, but what he finally did. Not the talk, but the walk.

Only that was not the part of the story that got Jesus killed! What got him killed was the second part, when he told the religious establishment of his time which brother they were.

Twenty-Sixth Sunday in Ordinary Time

They were the "yes" brothers who said all the right things, and stood for the right things, but who wouldn't DO the right things God asked them to do. They thought they were doing the right things by the strict interpretation of their religious rules and observances. But Jesus criticized them for their lack of compassion toward those oppressed by their habit of putting their laws and traditions ahead of persons.

On one level, this is one more story about hypocrisy. Hypocrisy has always been the number one charge leveled against religious people—that we say one thing and do another! That we promise on Sunday to love one another and then find any number of ways to hurt one another, or just plain ignore one another, on Monday.

So, it's tempting to reduce today's Gospel parable to what is obvious. Yes, "actions speak louder than words." But there's more to the story than that. We hear: "A man had two sons. He came to the first and said, 'Son, go out and work in the vineyard today.'

"And he answered, 'I will not.' But afterward he changed his mind and went."

It's easy to slide over the phrase "afterward he changed his mind." The biblical word for that is *REPENTANCE*!

When you read through the Gospels, you can't help but notice how often Jesus speaks about repentance. In fact, the first thing you hear him say in the Gospels of Matthew and Mark is this: "Repent, for the kingdom of heaven is at hand" (Matthew 4:17 and Mark 1:15). That was his very first sermon.

But what does that mean?

What does it mean to repent? Perhaps the best image of repentance is that of the first son in this story today. He was marching away from work in the vineyard, but then he turned around and walked back in the other direction. To repent is to realize that we have to change the direction our lives have been taking. But most of us don't like change, really. We put up a lot of resistance to change from the moment of birth on.

Whenever we feel settled and secure, we prefer to stay put. Why move? Things are fine the way they are. Besides, the unfamiliar is threatening. So, we stay put. And then it's easy to become complacent and intolerant of people who may think and react differently than I do.

Jesus came preaching change. He came with a new and revolutionary message to a people who were not disposed to hear it.

In the Prologue to his Gospel, John writes: "He came to what was his own, but his own people did not accept him" (John 1:11). I think this is one of the saddest verses in the Gospels!

The religious leaders of Christ's time were the older son of the parable. They were too self-satisfied to change. They thought they had all the right answers. And that they were doing all the right things. There was no NEED for them to change.

God gives us a wonderful image in the Book of Jeremiah of how he would like us to be. "Be with me like clay in the hands of a potter," God tells us (18:6). God wants to mold us and refine us like a potter molds and refines a clay dish he is making. Can any of us say: "That doesn't apply to me. I don't need to change"?

I often think of John Henry Newman's commentary that "to live is to change, and to be perfect is to have changed often." Aren't those wonderful words? "To live is to change," and to grow…"and to be perfect is to have changed often."

What changes might God be calling me to make at this time in my life? Are there habits, routines, that need changing? Is it time to forgive someone? To change spending habits? To become more socially conscious? To take better care of my health? To pray more?

Change can be difficult. Change takes time. But change starts with the DECISION to change. Is God calling me to make that decision? Is this the time? And if not now, when?

TWENTY-SEVENTH SUNDAY IN ORDINARY TIME

First Reading: Isaiah 5:1–7
Responsorial Psalm: 80
Second Reading: Philippians 4:6–9
Gospel: Matthew 21:33–43

❧

This morning, and for the past two Sundays, Matthew gives us one of the parables of Jesus to think about. His parables are sometimes thinly disguised criticisms of the religious authorities of his time, and of their abuse of power. And that's certainly true of today's story addressed to the chief priests and rabbis. It was parables like this that put Jesus on a collision course with the Jewish religious establishment.

The story he tells today is about real people, and real events in Jewish history. It's a chilling story, really! It's a story about hatred, violence, and murder. And part of that story is about Jesus himself. The owner's son in the story is seized, dragged out of the vineyard, and murdered. In a matter of a few days from the time he told this story, Jesus himself will be taken out of Jerusalem and murdered.

On one level, this parable is a strong indictment against the religious leadership of God's beloved vineyard, Israel. They had repeatedly rejected the prophets who came before Jesus, and now they were rejecting Jesus himself.

On another level, it's about the power of evil at work in the world and in the human heart. It's about the frightening capacity we have to deeply harm one another. We see so much suffering and pain in our world today. So many threats to world peace. So much greed. So much violence. So much hatred and suspicion. The array of moral and social evils that parade before our eyes and across our TV screens can easily lead us to question whether God is really running the world!

I'm reminded of a verse from the hymn that's so popular in many Baptist churches: "He's got the whole wide world in his hands!"

You may wonder about that sometimes! Does God really have the whole wide world in his hands? You know, there was a theory going around in the seventeenth century that acknowledged God as the Creator of the universe—but a God who then walked off and let it run by itself. Much like a watchmaker can go off and leave the watch running.

That's an understanding of God I'm sure some people have in every generation—people who say: "Yes, there's a God, but he's an absentee God." "God created the world, but then left us on our own." Otherwise, wouldn't God be protecting us from major evils? From earthquakes and hurricanes and famine? From premature and tragic death?

What the parable is saying is that good people, innocent people, are often not protected from these evils—not protected from suffering and gross injustice. And, of course, that includes Jesus himself. He is the preeminent victim of unjust suffering.

What's often hard for us to accept is that God has never promised a life that's trouble free, or evil free. What God has promised is to be with us in any trouble that comes to us.

And what God has proven is that God is stronger than evil, and that God can bring good out of evil.

That's the message here! And it's critically important!

We Christians can disagree on many things, on a variety of religious issues—but not on this one! This is fundamental and nonnegotiable. Our God is the God of the impossible—who can take something that's dead and buried, and bring it to life again! A dead job. A dead relationship. A dead person.

Notice in the parable today that the owner of the vineyard, God, does, in fact, retain control of the vineyard despite the poor care the farmers have given it. The owner's plans for the vineyard do get carried out! In the end, the vineyard does bear fruit!

We're being asked to believe that nothing can stop the vineyard from producing sweet grapes—not hatred, not violence, not murder, not greed, not anything!

Listen again to St. Paul's advice today in our second reading.

My brothers and sisters, have no anxiety at all, but in everything, by prayer and petition, with thanksgiving, make your requests known to God. Then the peace of God that surpasses all understanding will guard your hearts and minds in Christ Jesus.

TWENTY-EIGHTH SUNDAY IN ORDINARY TIME

First Reading: Isaiah 25:6–10a
Responsorial Psalm: 23
Second Reading: Philippians 4:12–14, 19–20
Gospel: Matthew 22:1–14 or 22:1–10

❧

After every Gospel reading, we conclude with the words "The Gospel of the Lord," or "The Good News of the Lord." But sometimes the good news doesn't sound all that good! And the Gospel this morning is an example of that.

It's cloaked in a parable we may not like very much and that sounds like bad news! If that's your reaction, you don't have to apologize. Matthew has woven together two parables here—both of them quite strange. And if they raise questions for you, I can't blame you!

Matthew's story has to be read in its context—the way we should always read Scripture, and particularly this passage today. It comes out of the context of a bitter first-century struggle between the Jewish people who believed that Jesus was the Messiah foretold in the Jewish Scriptures and those who were just as convinced he was not. The Gospel reflects that conflict in an allegory where you have to look carefully to find any good news at all!

What should surprise us most is that the story portrays God

as a vengeful king who believes in capital punishment! He sends an army to kill the people who have murdered his servants. He orders his troops to burn down their city. This is Matthew's veiled reference to the destruction of Jerusalem in the year AD 70. And then, at the very end of the story, the king banishes into darkness the poor fellow who had been hurried into the party from the street, and who couldn't possibly be properly dressed for the occasion.

This calls out for more explanation than I want to give in a Sunday homily. Because this is entirely unlike anything we want to believe about God! Because it's entirely unlike everything we know about Jesus! And Jesus remains the best source of our knowledge about God—the perfect image of what God is like, and the best standard by which we measure the message of the Scriptures.

And the picture we get of Jesus in the New Testament is not of an angry, volatile, vindictive person—still less some military commander who would deliberately plan the destruction of his enemy.

Juliana of Norwich, a theologian of the late fourteenth century, goes so far as to say that it is impossible for God to be angry! Impossible because anger and friendship are two contraries, two opposites. She writes: "I see no kind of wrath in God. Neither briefly nor for long. For if God could be angry, we would neither have life, nor place, nor being."

In fact, the Jesus of the Gospels is the most tender, loving person we could possibly imagine: a combination of mother, father, brother, sister, husband, wife, counselor, best friend…the ONE person you can absolutely depend on, the one who understands you completely. The one who will never, under any circumstances, let you down, or abandon you. And even if there's never been such a person in your life, you can surely imagine what he or she would be like: your friend in the fullest sense. The one who has faith in you no matter what…the one who knows just what methods to use to keep you from harming yourself.

When we take a close look at the story today, we discover that God is very eager for our friendship. Do you ever think of God in that way? Surely there are times in your life when you long for God, but do you ever think that God longs for you? Do you ever think that God diligently seeks you out? That God is passionately concerned for your happiness? And that your happiness is God's happiness?

In this parable today, God is the determined seeker. The king sends his servants out—not just once, but three times—to recruit guests for his banquet. It is a banquet Isaiah in that first reading today describes as "a feast of rich food and choice wines"—no bread and water survival food, but sumptuous food and drink, symbolic of the abundant life Jesus is offering.

It's hard to believe that people would turn down such an invitation! And for such feeble reasons! For the reason that I'm too busy, and that it's too much trouble to rearrange my schedule. And besides, I have the laundry to do and groceries to buy and the dog to walk. We do that! We have all kinds of things we put ahead of God in our life.

But in the story—even though the people invited may not be all that interested in the party—still the king wants very much to have them there! The parable is saying that God's love is like that! It's strong and determined. It pursues us. Even when we have excuses to avoid it. That's the first piece of good news this morning!

The second piece of good news is that God's love is not exclusive. It embraces everyone! Exclusiveness is a dangerous thing because of what it allows us to do to those who are excluded. It allows us to consider others unworthy and unfit. And then the way is open to discrimination and bigotry, to persecution and ethnic cleansing. There is too much of that going on in our world today! The problem with considering some as chosen is that others then become unchosen, ruled out.

The Jewish people in the time of Jesus got a big surprise when Jesus began to preach to them that their God loved others as much as he loved them! It was even a bigger surprise for them to learn that God loves sinners as well as the virtuous! I'm sure you noticed that the king invites the good AND the bad to his party. He welcomes them BOTH!

Twenty-Eighth Sunday in Ordinary Time

I want to ask you this morning: Do you really believe in this kind of God? Do you really believe in a passionately loving God whose arms are always wide open? Never closed to anyone? Never closed to you? Never, ever closed to you? If you are a Christian, that has to be your picture of God!

But trust in this understanding of God can only build very slowly in us. It's wonderfully expressed by St. Paul in that second reading today. Paul says he has known ups and downs in his life, but he's learned how to cope with both. "I can do all things in God who strengthens me," he says. Another translation of that puts it this way: "I am ready for anything—through the strength of the One who lives within me" (J.B. Phillips).

A false, unreal kind of religion tries to have you believe something like this: "Fear not. Trust in God, and God will see to it that none of the things you fear will happen to you." You have to be very wary about such a message! Authentic religion teaches us something quite different—more like: "Fear not. The things you are afraid of may well happen to you, but they're nothing to be afraid of!"

Do you see the difference? It's a big difference! And it comes from trust in a God who can't possibly be wrathful or harbor grudges, and who very much wants you to be part of the great banquet that's a symbol for his own life shared with us—here and now, especially through the sacraments, but most fully, later.

TWENTY-NINTH SUNDAY IN ORDINARY TIME

First Reading: Isaiah 45:1, 4–6
Responsorial Psalm: 96
Second Reading: 1 Thessalonians 1:1–5b
Gospel: Matthew 22:15–21

✣

There are some people who refuse to enter into any discussion of religion or politics! In a way, I can understand their caution. Both topics—religion and politics—are big time. And most people have strong opinions about them.

Some of the issues involve the question that comes up in the Gospel today: the question of taxes to the secular government. On the surface, the question put to Jesus was simple enough, but it was a loaded question. "Is it lawful to pay the census tax to Caesar or not?" If Jesus were to answer "No," he could be accused of sedition and subject to arrest by the Romans. If he were to answer "Yes," he'd alienate the people who naturally resented paying taxes to a foreign and oppressive government. As so often happened to him, it was a trap!

So, he doesn't answer the question. Instead, he asks to see a coin.

Archeologists tell us that coins of that time had the image of Caesar Augustus, the reigning Emperor, much like our own money carries the image of past presidents.

Twenty-Ninth Sunday in Ordinary Time

You may recall that the teaching of the Old Testament is that when something bears the image of another, it belongs to the one whose image it carries. So, when the Book of Genesis says that man and woman are made in the image of God, this means God's image is branded on you and me! And we belong to God! And to no other!

That's why that first reading was selected for today. "I am the Lord, and there is no other," God tells Isaiah. We need to hear that! Because we have the stubborn tendency—don't we?—to put other gods, false gods, in place of the one true God.

So, Jesus asks them to show him a coin: "Whose image is on this coin?" he wants to know.

And they answer: "Caesar's."

Then comes the often-quoted response of Jesus: "Then give to Caesar what belongs to Caesar, and to God what belongs to God."

This was not a clever dodge on his part! Rather, it's a confrontation to his questioners. The really important part of the answer is that second part. "Give to God what belongs to God." That is to say: Give God yourself, your whole self! Because you belong to God. You are God's coin, so to speak, minted by God.

Jesus is summoning the Pharisees to a deeper relationship with God. He's not setting up a false dichotomy between God and secular authority, between religion and politics. He's not telling us: "Don't mix religion and politics. Keep Church and state, God and Caesar, separate."

That's what some people would like these words of Jesus to mean, and that's what some have claimed they mean. I'm sure you've heard people say things like: "The Church has no business getting involved in political affairs." "The Church should stick to spiritual things and not meddle in secular matters!"

The Church is supposed to content itself with prayer and worship, with baptisms, weddings, and funerals. With what is sometimes jestingly referred to as "hatching, matching and dispatching."

Some cite the First Amendment to our Constitution as the basis for a strict separation of Church and state, of religion and politics. You remember the wording of that amendment: "Congress shall make no law respecting the establishment of religion, or prohibiting the free exercise thereof." In other words, Congress is not to favor one religion over another. However, that doesn't mean religion has nothing to say to the state. It doesn't claim, as some people do, that churches have no right to comment on what is regarded as a political matter.

In fact, the First Amendment gives to all citizens, and that includes religious leaders, the right to represent their grievances to the government. Religious leaders not only have the right to comment on human affairs, but they also have the duty to examine human affairs in the light of their own religious beliefs. They have the obligation to guide us in matters such as modern warfare, the death penalty, abortion, housing for the homeless, just wages—just to mention some of the crucial ethical issues affecting human life and dignity.

We can never be seduced by those who want the Church sidelined from the mainstream of the debates that shape the way we live and the values we share and the laws we draft. If the Church should show disinterest or impartiality in any of this, it would be unfaithful to the very things Jesus lived for.

THIRTIETH SUNDAY IN ORDINARY TIME

First Reading: Exodus 22:20–26
Responsorial Psalm: 18
Second Reading: 1 Thessalonians 1:5c–10
Gospel: Matthew 22:34–40

❧

Not long ago, I was speaking to a lawyer from California, and she was telling me about some outdated and silly laws still on the books there. Did you know that in 1930 a law was passed in Ontario, California, forbidding roosters crowing within the city limits? And that in Los Angeles you could not bathe two babies in the same tub at the same time?

Silly laws, aren't they? Yet when they passed that law in Ontario, California, there really was a rooster problem that had gotten out of hand, and they were disturbing people's sleep. Let's presume that most laws are written for a serious reason. But after time passes, some laws that were once needed can become antiquated and no longer applicable.

The same thing can happen in religion. Some laws and customs, after the passage of time, can become antiquated. In the time of Jesus, there were 613 religious laws. Imagine that! Imagine trying to balance 613 claims on the way you live your life!

Some were called "light laws" because they were of lesser significance. For example, laws concerning dietary rules and cleansing rituals. But others were called "heavy" because these were laws of importance. For example, the treatment of parents, dealings with neighbors, and observance of the Sabbath. The great religious leaders of the time were often asked by sincere religious people to prioritize the laws, and to name the most important. This was so people could be helped to live better lives. But different religious leaders had differing opinions, and they would argue for their point of view.

We hear such a situation in today's Gospel passage. A scholar of the religious law asks Jesus his opinion. "Teacher, which commandment in the law is the greatest?" We're told the question is not sincere and that the scholar was out to trap Jesus.

Jesus looked into his own heart, and he knew instinctively what the greatest commandment is. And so, he quotes from the Book of Deuteronomy: "You shall love the Lord your God with all your heart, with all your soul, and with all your mind." And from the Book of Leviticus, he quotes: "You shall love your neighbor as yourself." Jesus joins the two into one! For him, they're inseparable. You can't speak of one without the other.

And it calls us to have God as our center. Nothing is more important than this. Nothing is more important than our personal relationship with God! And the way we know that God is our center is by showing love to one another. You may remember that St. John, in his first letter, puts this very strongly. "Those who say, 'I love God,' and hate their brothers or sisters are liars; for those who do not love a brother or sister whom they have seen, cannot love God whom they have not seen," John writes (1 John 4:20, NRSV).

But then the question comes up: how can love be commanded? We usually don't think about love in this way. When people love one another, it's not because they've been commanded to do so. Our idea of love is often very inadequate and limited to a feeling, an emotion. But the love Jesus is speaking about here is not a feeling! We can't produce a feeling, however hard we try! Love is not principally a feeling, though that's the popular misconception celebrated over and over in poetry and love songs. Love is a decision—an act of the will—rather than a feeling! A deliberate decision, a choice to act lovingly—whether we feel like it or not. Feeling may enter into it, or it may not. I may like you, or I may dislike you. That's not important when it comes to living out this commandment of love. Liking someone is a matter of temperament, of personality, and of circumstances. To love you is to act in your best interests—even if it's at some cost to my personal feelings, or my convenience. Even if I don't like you, I can behave toward you in a decent, respectful way. When Jesus speaks about loving, it's the way we treat people. It's concrete behavior that he's speaking about, not a feeling!

This Gospel today is among the best-known parts of the Bible because it says so much in so few words. And truly, it's the heart of our faith, the core of the Christian gospel. It's so central to the teaching of Jesus that it's quoted by Matthew, Mark, and Luke so that we don't miss it. And it doesn't take a degree in theology or a scholar of religious law to understand what it means. It's the answer to a question all of us must ask: What do I have to do to lead a morally good life?

But it's much more than that too. It's the answer to the bigger question: What is life all about? How do I live a meaningful life? How can I be happy and fulfilled?

The answer Jesus gives is love. Loving God and one another is why we have been born! It's what we're here on earth for! And the Eucharist we share here today is meant to be a powerful help to us for that. May it help us in the coming weeks to raise our minds and hearts to God more, and to act more lovingly toward that neighbor whom I feel is so irritating!

THIRTY-FIRST SUNDAY IN ORDINARY TIME

First Reading: Malachi 1:14b—2:2b, 8–10
Responsorial Psalm: 131
Second Reading: 1 Thessalonians 2:7b–9, 13
Gospel: Matthew 23:1–12

※

S omeone once said of Jesus that he came to comfort the afflicted and to afflict the comfortable! Nowhere in the Gospels is this more evident than in the twenty-third chapter of Matthew that we begin hearing today. Jesus is just getting warmed up here! You have to read on in this chapter of Matthew to get the full force of Christ's words aimed at unsettling the spiritually comfortable. He takes to task some of the professional religious people of his time for their pride. For considering themselves morally superior to others. This shows itself in their seeking first places of honor and outward signs of respect—insisting on titles for themselves like "Rabbi" and "Master." Not that titles are wrong. But what turns them wrong is when people take them seriously as signs of personal excellence and consider themselves better than others.

One of the recurrent messages of Scripture is that God is not revealed to people who consider themselves important, worthy, wise, or powerful. This attitude is ridiculous before God! Because it belies the truth of the human situation. God is revealed to those who know themselves to be needy, dependent, loved by God out of the divine goodness, and not because of human merit of any kind. This is painfully difficult for us to accept! It's difficult to accept that all we have, and all we are, is pure gift from God. We're not better than others because we're more educated, or more successful in the eyes of the world.

Here today Jesus tells his Jewish audience to listen to what their religious leaders are teaching them because their teaching comes from the Hebrew Scriptures. But he warns: "Don't follow them in what they do." Because they are all talk and no show! If you talk the talk, you ought to walk the walk, as the saying goes!

This is a stinging indictment to make about anyone—especially about people in positions of authority. After a while, you get fed up with words, and more words, that never materialize into anything. We get fed up with politicians who promise, but don't deliver. We get fed up with preachers who don't practice what they preach. Who would want to be treated by a heart doctor who is badly overweight and a chain smoker?

People who don't live what they preach are an embarrassment and a contradiction! Jesus denounces them as "hypocrites." That word: "hypocrite"—as you may know—comes from the Greek word meaning "actor." As in someone who is playing a role and pretending to be someone he's not. There are those who role-play at religion by living it on a merely external level.

But the practice of religion on a very safe and comfortable level, keeping the weightier claims of religion at arm's length, is not just a first-century problem. It's a perennial problem. The temptation is to what you might call "Christianity lite"—a Christianity without too many demands on me!

But there's something else out there—another phenomenon some people call hypocrisy, but which really isn't. I'm talking now about the person who does pretty well at practicing what he or she preaches, but not out of total conviction, or maybe with only minimal conviction. This person keeps up the formalities, says prayers, and goes to Mass routinely—not to appear good in the eyes of others, but to search and to hope.

This is the person who has a genuine difficulty about faith or practice. This person says: "How can I believe in a God who allows babies to be born with AIDS, and who permitted upwards of seventy thousand people to perish in the recent earthquake?"

This type of person also says: "How can I depend on God when my prayers for so long have gone unanswered? I go to church on Sundays, but I'm not sure anymore. So much has changed. What am I doing here? I don't think I really believe anymore! I feel like a hypocrite!"

But notice. This is something different! This is not the pride of hypocrisy. This is journey and search. This is the discipline of someone keeping up appearances, not to deceive and to win applause, but to get some kind of sign from God that God is there and really cares! These are people trying to be faithful even when they don't get anything out of it.

Such people are not hypocrites. They are searchers after truth! And they are beloved of God who is surely with them in their search.

Such people have a patron saint, I think, in the old man Simeon of Luke's Gospel—the man who for thirty years came to the temple every day looking for the Messiah— and who for thirty years went away disappointed. Who came out of hope and out of simple routine. Who eventually got bored, who got nothing out of being faithful. His was true worship, with the focus away from his own spiritual dryness and totally on the search for God. That's why eventually Simeon got to look into the face of the Messiah, to hold him in his arms, and to sing his great song of thanksgiving that Luke has preserved for us in the second chapter of his Gospel. One day it all came together for Simeon, as it will for all who keep on searching and waiting.

THIRTY-SECOND SUNDAY
IN ORDINARY TIME

First Reading: Wisdom 6:12–16
Responsorial Psalm: 63
Second Reading: 1 Thessalonians 4:13–18 or 4:13–14
Gospel: Matthew 25:1–13

✺

The first Christians fully expected Jesus to return very soon after his resurrection and ascension. And you couldn't blame them, really. At the end of his life, Jesus had frequently urged them to stay awake and be ready because he would be coming back at an hour they couldn't foresee.

In our second reading today, St. Paul, writes with the conviction that Jesus will return WITHIN PAUL'S OWN LIFETIME! And that a new creation, a renewed world, would begin. But the early Christians were eventually doomed to disappointment as the years went by, and Jesus was a no-show! Some began to wonder if he was coming back at all! And if so, when? And how were they to conduct themselves in the interim?

The Gospel parable today is Matthew's answer to this dilemma. It's aimed at those who were losing heart and giving up. He offers a parable from Jesus that basically warns his followers to be always ready. The Lord, like the bridegroom, will indeed come. But he will come when we least expect him. So don't be foolish. Be prepared!

For centuries, Christians have been reciting a Creed that proclaims: "He will come again to judge the living and the dead." And every now and then, people appear who claim to know exactly when Jesus is coming back! Such interest in the second coming of Jesus is still alive. And why not? Particularly now. We're in the midst of a worldwide epidemic that has killed over a million people? And still raging. We see that the planet is warming; sea levels are rising; earthquakes, hurricanes, and forest fires are becoming more common. Who could blame some people for thinking we might be drawing near the end of the world as predicted in Scripture?

And yet, it's more likely that we're still stuck in the in between time—with the "meanwhile." And until that second coming arrives—what shall we do in the meanwhile? Matthew's answer in the parable today gives us a way to manage "the meanwhile." He offers us two themes: "be prepared" and "be recognized."

First, be prepared—not only for the visitation of Jesus in death and judgment, but also—and especially—for his visitations in life! He comes especially in the sacraments. He comes when we're inspired to help those in need; he comes when we're moved to pray.

And then there are the more insistent attention getters: the beauty of a sunset; the falling-asleep-in-your-arms of your first child.

These are moments when God draws particularly near. Or, as the parable might say, when the bridegroom is here. If we stay awake to recognize these times, we would be prepared indeed. This is Matthew's first lesson.

The second important lesson from this parable is to live in such a way as to be recognized as one whom Jesus knows. The truly shocking words Jesus speaks here in this story are these: "Amen, I say to you, I do not know you." I don't think there could be any more terrifying words in all of Scripture! I shudder to hear them! Jesus not know me? A Catholic all my life? Why doesn't he know me?

A clue comes in another part of the Gospels when his mother and his relatives want to see him but can't get near because of the crowd. So, they send word to him, and finally someone near him says to Jesus: "Excuse me, but your mother and your brethren are here to see you."

But Jesus says for everyone to hear: "Who is my mother? Who are my brothers?...whoever does the will of my heavenly Father is my brother, and sister, and mother" (Matthew 12:48–50).

What makes us mother and brother and sister to Christ is our faith and good works—not a baptismal certificate from the church of my baptism!

This comes across quite pointedly in the parable where the foolish virgins ask the five wise ones to share some of their oil with them. And the five wise ones refuse! That sounds very selfish. But they're wiser than we may think. Christian tradition tells us that the oil stands for faith and good works. And these are simply not transferable. You can't borrow someone else's faith. You can't borrow another's good works. You have to respond to God yourself.

So, for us who live "in the meanwhile" time, Matthew left us this Jesus parable. Five of the bridesmaids stayed alert to welcome the groom. Five of the women were foolish. They never slowed down enough to listen for the whisperings of God, or to fill their lamps with faith and good works. They put their own selfish interests first. They had become strangers to Jesus, the bridegroom! And at the end, they may be destined to hear those terrifying words from him that none of us wants to hear: "I do not recognize you."

THIRTY-THIRD SUNDAY IN ORDINARY TIME

First Reading: Proverbs 31:10–13, 19–20, 30–31
Responsorial Psalm: 128
Second Reading: 1 Thessalonians 5:1–6
Gospel: Matthew 25:14–30 or 25:14–15, 19–21

☙

Two weeks from today we begin a new Church year with the First Sunday of Advent. In these final weeks, the Scripture readings are mostly about the end time, that unknown future time when Christ "will come again in glory to judge the living and the dead," in the words of the Creed we profess every Sunday. This is Matthew's concern in giving us this parable today.

But this is a tricky parable! And Scripture scholars caution us about it. They caution against identifying God too closely with the wealthy merchant who entrusted large amounts of his money to three of his servants and then goes on a long journey. The rich employer in the story is regarded as a hard and demanding man! But the Christian God is not! Our God is a God of love and mercy— not like the harsh boss in this story who demands that we produce in order to earn a reward. So, with that understood, what is the parable telling us?

Most of us would take it to mean that people should use their gifts and talents for the good of others. God gives different abilities to each of us, and God expects us to use them wisely and generously. But if that's the message, no one would be crucified for telling a story as inoffensive as that! We have to remember that this parable was told just a few days before the arrest and crucifixion of Jesus. Many scripture scholars believe the story was directed against the powerful religious aristocracy of the time, and that the Jewish religious leaders correspond to the third servant in the story. Because their one aim in life was to keep things as they were.

And then Jesus came along—with new ideas about God, about life, and about one's duties in life. And Jesus was not orthodox enough for them! So, they began to plot his death.

This is a reminder to us that in the Christian faith there has to be steady development. We believe that God is infinite. And that no one can ever get to the end of God. The riches of Christ are unsearchable. No one can exhaust them. This means that every generation should be penetrating deeper and deeper into the truth about God! Every one of us, all our life long, should be learning more and more about God!

In the life of the Church, there's something very wrong if, in a span of a hundred years, say, people have not learned more about the meaning of their religion! In my own life, there's something wrong if my faith remains where it was ten or twenty years ago. If my faith at age fifty is the same as it was at age twenty, I ought to be concerned! I think the parable today is a challenge to go deeper into our faith.

A few other things have to be noticed about this story today. The servants in the story were given different amounts of money. We're all born with different abilities, and the test is how we use the abilities we have. It's pointless to envy someone else's talent. What we have to do is make the best of our own!

The parable condemns the one who won't try! Very likely the third servant felt it was not worth trying. He had only one talent, and it didn't seem worthwhile trying to use it. Someone has said that "God doesn't want extraordinary people who do extraordinary things nearly so much as God wants ordinary people who do ordinary things extraordinarily well." Make no mistake about it. The functioning of the world depends on people with the one talent!

I think we can say this story is basically a story about trust. The rich businessman trusts each of his servants with large amounts of money. And then he vanishes. This was a risky thing for him to do! But we hear that the first two servants were enterprising and doubled their investment. The third servant is the key player in the story. He's crippled by fear and so he plays it safe. He buries the money. When his boss returns, he hands back the cash without loss. After all, putting money in the ground would be normal protection in an age without banks.

I think about this servant this morning. I'm concerned about him. Because I think in our world his name is legion! I'm thinking of the people for whom life is not so much a gift to be nurtured and developed, as it is a problem to be coped with. What about the person who may sit here this morning and realize that not only is there no great achievement, nothing splendid in her life, but that life is sour and empty. Or what about the life that is afraid…like the servant in our story today? Out of fear, the potential for a fuller life has been buried. Maybe you know people like that—with a deep distrust of life and a destructive attitude to what happens in life.

They're afraid of commitment and the risks that go along with commitment. They're afraid to love and be loved. They refuse to obligate themselves. They may call that "caution" or "prudence." But what it really is—they don't want to get hurt! But this is no way to live! Because life is too precious a gift. Life needs to be invested in, and risks have to be taken!

A priest friend who works in a long-term care facility has told me that the saddest people he sees are those who can find no meaning in their lives because they didn't really live! They minded their own business. They didn't get involved. They've been hurt by life, and they spend a good deal of time asking, "Why me?" Life was breaking in all around them, and they were always on the wrong side of the door from the party! It reminds me of a Billy Joel song called "An Innocent Man" where he sang about how people sometimes stay away from a door with the fear of it opening up.

This Gospel parable today is about being prepared for the coming again of Jesus at the end of time—on judgment day. But it's much more than that, too! It's about being committed to living fully NOW. It's about trusting God, trusting that God really wants to share life with me as fully as possible! There are no restrictions on the joy God wants me to have! What the rich man in the parable really wants is to see his servants' happiness grow as they discover their gifts multiplying! The question for you and me this morning is: Do I really believe the Lord when he tells me, in so many different ways, that he wants nothing but happiness for me—happiness multiplied?

CHRIST THE KING
(Last Sunday in Ordinary Time)

First Reading: Ezekiel 34:11–12, 15–17
Responsorial Psalm: 23
Second Reading: 1 Corinthians 15:20–26, 28
Gospel: Matthew 25:31–46

❦

One of the oldest titles the Church has given to Christ is "King of Kings." I have to confess I don't find "King" an appealing image for Jesus! It may have been meaningful at an earlier time in history, but today most countries don't have kings anymore. Our own country, and many others, have never had a king! When we hear the word *King*, we usually think of someone quite removed from ordinary people, someone of great power and wealth and privilege who has a lot to say about the lives of people under him in his kingdom. Most of our ancestors came to this country to get away from kings!

So, Christ a king? Well, yes. But not in the way we imagine a king to be!

We have a clue to the kind of king Christ is in the main Scripture readings today. The picture in that first reading from the prophet Ezekiel is not of a king with a crown on his head, but of a

186

shepherd with a staff in his hand. And this shepherd king speaks out about the way he rules.

Listen again: "I myself will look after and tend my sheep. I will rescue them from every place where they were scattered. The strayed I will bring back. The injured I will bind up. The sick I will heal." That doesn't sound like a king speaking. This is more like a tender mother or father speaking.

And we see this in the Gospel, too. This is an extraordinary Gospel! In Matthew, these are the very last words of Jesus to his disciples a few days before he was arrested and led away to be crucified. The scene here is of the Last Judgment, at some future time that's hidden from us now. But the teaching is far more concerned with the here-and-now of Christian life than with judgment on the last day.

The king in this judgment scene is a total surprise! He identifies with the needy, with the least in his kingdom. Usually, kings ally themselves with the most powerful. But not this king. Here there's a complete inversion of all earthly notions of power! Here the king is not in some distant place far above the pain and the suffering of the world. Here he identifies with the suffering!

That makes me consider the example of Mother Teresa of Calcutta—St. Teresa of Calcutta. She said that we must seek Jesus in the poor, downtrodden, and suffering people of the world. She says we find him there, in our own time.

That conviction of hers challenges all our notions of power and lordship. Here is a king who stands the very idea of kingship on its head! No other religion in the world dares to speak of God in this way—as hiding behind the faces of the needy! What a deep mystery that is.

But this isn't the only element of surprise in this story. Both the sheep and the goats—the virtuous and the wicked—are taken by surprise! "When did we see you hungry and feed you?" the good sheep will say. They seem to be unaware that they're doing anything particularly praiseworthy. But that's the way with love, isn't it? You forget yourself in loving and caring for another person. That person becomes more important than you.

Often, I find myself complimenting parents on the love they're showing to their children. And they usually answer with something like: "We're not doing anything special! We're doing what any loving parents would do." They don't even realize the good they're doing! It's the same way with the ordinary kindnesses we do for one another in the course of a day.

This Gospel is not just meant for individual Christians—not just meant for you and me! It also calls on the Christian community, indeed on all nations, to respond to the needy. And that's a serious responsibility. We look around the world today and see such enormous poverty: people desperately needing clean drinking water and medicine for the aged and very young; needing food in famine and war-stricken countries; needing help; and in cleaning up the air and preserving natural resources.

I can imagine Jesus saying to the nations gathered before him today: "I was hungry, and you did not give me seeds to plant crops. I was thirsty, and your industries fouled my streams and rivers. I was a stranger, and you sent me back to my native land. I was sick, and you refused to lower the price of prescription drugs." I can imagine him saying, "You are doing this to me."

Jesus is teaching here in this parable what even religious-minded people are slow to learn. He teaches that God seems less impressed by what we do for him than by what we do for one another! I'm reminded of the words of Jesus to Peter in John's Gospel. "Do you love me, Peter?...Then, feed my lambs....Feed my sheep" (John 21:15–17).

Sometimes people wonder if they really love God. And I think the best way to find out is to ask myself: "How much love and kindness am I showing to the people at my elbow?"

SOLEMNITIES AND FEASTS THAT MAY DISPLACE ORDINARY TIME SUNDAYS

THE PRESENTATION
(February 2)

First Reading: Malachi 3:1–4
Responsorial Psalm: 24
Second Reading: Hebrews 2:14–18
Gospel: Luke 2:22–40 or 2:22–32

⁓

You've heard of people being bumped on airplane flights. Someone comes along with a higher claim to your seat, and you get moved. Well, something like that happens today with this Mass. Today we don't follow the normal sequence of prayers and Scripture readings for Sunday. Instead, we have the Mass of February 2, the Feast of the Presentation of Jesus in the temple as an infant.

It's exactly forty days after Christmas today! And in some ways, the Gospel story today is another Epiphany story. Another manifestation of who Jesus is. The question of his identity, of just who Jesus was, was a huge issue in the early centuries of the Church. Simeon and Anna, under the inspiration of the Holy Spirit, they recognize the infant Jesus as the long-awaited Messiah—destined, as Simeon says, for "the fall and rise of many in Israel." Another identification of who he is, is made in our second reading this morning—and I'm quoting here—"he had to become like [us] in every way"—"yet without sin"—this letter to the Hebrews says a little further on! (Hebrews 2:17; 4:15).

Jesus, the promised Messiah, fully human, and like us in every way, but without sin!

As I think about the liturgical year that lies ahead of us, and the many ways Jesus will reveal himself through the Gospel stories, I wonder what would happen if I could pass out half sheets of paper to everyone here, and I said that we'd take a couple of minutes for each of us to write down, in about two hundred words, what we would say to people who knew nothing about Christianity—and who wanted to know what Christians believe. What would we say? We have a story to tell. How would we write that story in about two hundred words? What are the main parts to our story?

Well, one way to do it would simply be to write the Nicene Creed which we'll all profess together right after I finish speaking here! That would be one way. But here is another way, in less philo- sophical and theological language. You might say something like this:

"We believe that God created the whole universe. We believe that Jesus Christ, conceived in Mary's womb by the power of the Holy Spirit, is fully human and fully God. That he lived in this world, died, and was brought through death to the destiny we all share. We believe that the risen Jesus has gifted us with God the Holy Spirit, and that we have God's own life within us.

We believe that God is specially present to the Church. We believe that at every Eucharist the whole movement of Jesus giving himself to the Father, finally in his dying on the cross, is made pres- ent to us so that we can enter into that movement unto death. And we look forward to the time when all will be well, and all creation will come home to God."

This is another way of doing a sort of summary—in our own words—of what we Christians believe. We have a great story to tell! A beautiful, hopeful story. And we need to know the story, think about the story, and keep it before us.

There are a few things to notice about the Christian story. Notice that it begins with God and creation. That's where the Creed begins. We believe that this is not a rotten, throw-away universe.

God became part of it through the birth of Jesus. And, through the gift of the Holy Spirit, God remains very active in the world. There's a goodness in the world that outweighs all the evil put together! There's a light in the world that shines in the darkness, and the darkness will not overcome it.

The Eucharist is also critical to this story. And the Eucharist is not simply a remembrance of what Jesus once did. The action of Jesus—offering himself to the Father—is made present to us at every Eucharist, and we have the opportunity to enter into it.

I think we have to acknowledge that our core beliefs are not that many! And they're not all that complicated. It's simply that they verge on the unbelievable! They seem too good to be true! But that's what we believe, and that's what we profess every time we pray the Creed. If we take each of these beliefs and think hard about them, we're filled with wonder and awe! Because we hold astounding truths! For instance, every time we gather for Mass, we believe the glorified body of Jesus becomes present to us here as food for our nourishment. As youngsters would say, "It's awesome."

Now it could happen that someone writing down a brief summary of what we Christians believe might begin by listing what we're supposed to do, or not do. They might say, "Christians are people who are supposed to do such and such....or not do such and such." They'd start with morality. But I think that would be the wrong beginning!

We act differently because we see differently! And it's seeing that makes all the difference! Please notice, by the way, that there are no do's and don'ts in the Creed! No morality in the Creed. Just profound truths, profound beliefs.

When we believe these truths, then we live differently! We live differently because we see the world differently. We see the meaning of life differently. And it's the seeing that makes all the difference!

We have a great story to tell! And it's not that complicated. At every Mass we celebrate the whole story. First, there's the liturgy of the Word. We listen to the story as it's told in the Bible. And then follows the liturgy of the Eucharist. At the offertory part of the Mass, we place ourselves on the altar with the bread and the wine, and we ask to be transformed along with them. And then we receive the bread and the cup. We receive the glorified body of the risen Lord at Communion. And we are one with God.

May the year that lies ahead of us strengthen our faith in the marvelous good news that is the Christian story!

ST. JOSEPH, HUSBAND OF MARY
(March 19)

First Reading: 2 Samuel 7:4–5a, 12–14a, 16
Responsorial Psalm: 89
Second Reading: Romans 4:13, 16–18, 22
Gospel: Matthew 1:16, 18–21, 24a or Luke 2:41–51a

Imagine how Joseph must have felt at the beginning of today's Gospel! His dreams have all been smashed. The woman he loves has betrayed him. She has gotten pregnant by someone else. He had to make a choice. He can either have her taken to the edge of town and stoned to death, or he can divorce her quietly.

Joseph chooses the more merciful alternative. Because after a divorce, in this culture, Mary would be treated as someone dead. Never again would her name be mentioned in Nazareth! But before he acts, Joseph dares to dream once more. In his dream, an angel appears to him and explains the pregnancy to him.

And so, Joseph completes his engagement to Mary by bringing her into his home and accepting the child as his. He trusts God enough to allow God's plans to guide his own.

St. Augustine once wrote that "faith is to believe what we do not see. And the reward of faith is to see what we believe." I think that's a good description of St. Joseph's life!

It's regretful that we have no record of the relationship Jesus had with Joseph. That loss is especially tragic in our culture where many men deeply feel the absence of their fathers. What lessons might we have learned had we known more? Well, perhaps we can deduce two things from today's Scriptures.

First, from the prophecy of Samuel, I imagine Joseph taught Jesus a love of his ancestors. He must have rooted his son in the prophecies and practices of the faith that grounded his own life. Joseph taught Jesus what it meant to be a Jew, one of God's chosen people who trusted in God's promise to be with them—at their side—in every adversity.

And secondly, in accord with the Letter to the Romans, I imagine Joseph taught his son the full meaning of faith—belief that hopes against hope! I like to believe the faith and hope that sustained Jesus on the cross was first nurtured by Joseph. Joseph must have given his son roots from which to grow and taught him endurance against life's hardships. Not a bad description of fatherhood!

THE ANNUNCIATION
(March 25)

First Reading: Isaiah 7:10–14; 8:10
Responsorial Psalm: 40
Second Reading: Hebrews 10:4–10
Gospel: Luke 1:26–38

❧

"I have come to do your will, O Lord."
"To do your will is my delight."
"Let your will be done."

These verses from today's Readings ring in my ears today. As Mary speaks her "fiat"—"let your will be done"—I think of the petition in the Lord's Prayer: "Thy will be done on earth as it is in heaven." And I think of the response of Jesus in Gethsemane: "Not my will but your will be done" (Luke 22:42). This was the driving force in our Lord's life. We know this especially from St. John's Gospel. Again and again, Jesus says in that Gospel that the only reason he has come into this world is to do the will of his Father. In the Sunday's Gospel of ten days ago, the account of our Lord's meeting with the Samaritan woman at the well, we heard Jesus tell his disciples: "My food is to do the will of Him who sent me" (John 4:34).

It is this doing and accepting of the will of God that sums up the essence of religion. I've realized that for a long time, but it strikes me today with renewed importance. I recall what St. Therese of the

Child Jesus wrote, at the end of her autobiography, that Jesus does not ask great deeds from us. All he wants is self-surrender.

It seems to me I'm prepared for this only if I'm ready to accept the insecurity of life and to follow the lead of God without knowing exactly where God is taking me. And I sense there's a lot of resistance in me to that. I'd much prefer to arrange the events of life myself. I sometimes think I'd be a lot better off if I could determine my own future. Sometimes I think I would rather pray: "Thy will be changed" rather than "Thy will be done."

And I know where this is coming from. It's coming from a deep-rooted self-seeking. I have the feeling that too often I'm living my life not primarily to please God, but to please myself without displeasing Him. In ways subtle and in ways sometimes obvious, it is I who come first, and the Lord functions for me as a restraint, a corrective upon too much self-satisfaction, too much self-fulfillment. I know this must change before I can see God.

As we celebrate Mary's self-surrender to the will of God with this feast today, I pray that she intercedes for us in our desire to seek God's will above our own, and whatever that may be, to surrender to it as soon as it's plainly manifested within us.

THE BIRTH OF JOHN THE BAPTIST
(June 24)

First Reading: Isaiah 49:1–6
Responsorial Psalm: 139
Second Reading: Acts 13:22–26
Gospel: Luke 1:57–66, 80

If you were asked to list the ten saints you most admired, my guess is that John the Baptist would not be on that list! If people today think of John the Baptist at all, it's usually as a head on a platter! This is how he is depicted in one of the three mosaics in the baptistery of our own church. We give the Baptist an entire Sunday today—displacing the usual Sunday readings—because today is his birthday. Well, it's really not his birthday! We have no idea when that was. We celebrate it on June 24 each year for a symbolic reason. It's something like the British celebrating Queen Elizabeth's birthday—not in April, when she was born, but in June—when there's a chance for better weather in England.

With John, it's not the weather. With John, the date is a symbol of light! Because in our hemisphere now, the darkness has diminished, and the light is full and bright. Just last Wednesday, we had the first day of summer and the longest period of sunlight in the northern hemisphere—fifteen hours! In this week of long days of light, it's the Baptist's role to announce the coming of The Great Light of the World, Jesus Christ.

John's role in salvation history was to point out Jesus as the one for whom the world was waiting. In the second reading today from the Acts of the Apostles, Paul, speaking of John says: "He would say: You think that I am the one you're waiting for. I am not. But there is one coming who is greater than I, whose sandals I am not worthy to unfasten."

And when the Jewish authorities sent priests and Levites to ask John who he is, he answered: "No, I am not the Messiah…I'm just the voice of one crying in the desert: prepare a straight way for the Lord" (John 1:20, 23). John had no illusions about his subsidiary role!

People would line up at the Jordan River to submit to his baptism—a ritual washing John did for them as they repented of their sins. When Jesus arrived on the scene to be baptized, John's message takes a new turn: "Behold, the Lamb of God," he tells them. "This is the one I've been telling you about. It's he who takes away the sins of the world" (cf. John 1: 29–30). "He must increase; I must decrease" (John 3:30).

This great Jewish prophet and contemporary of Jesus was who he was, and that's all he was. He had no need to be anything more than he really was. He had no need to play the leading role in the drama of salvation. He had no need to cry out, "Me, Me." He could point beyond himself and rejoice in another. "He must increase; I must decrease."

I'm reminded of when the Second Vatican Council opened. Pope John XXIII encouraged the Church in Council to resist the temptation to point to itself. Early on, when it looked like the Council was not heeding the pope's advice, one of the Council Fathers rose to the floor and complained: "Why is it," he said, "that when we, the world's bishops, speak about the Church, we point to ourselves, as though WE were the Church. We are not the Church. The People of God is the Church."

That bishop's intervention had a profound effect on the Council Fathers. And eventually "People of God" became the Council's working definition of the Church. The Church is not the Vatican! It's not the local bishop or even the bishops of the country.

The Church is the entire People of God!

Some Church historians have referred to that as the "Copernican Revolution of Vatican II"—meaning: the sun doesn't revolve around us! The hierarchy in Council was pointing to something greater than itself: "The People of God." And that became the Council's answer to the question: Who Am I?

A second question is asked in the Church document some consider the Council's most important document entitled "The Church in the Modern World" (*Gaudium et spes*). It asks the question: "What should the Church—the People of God—be doing?" The Council gave a very simple and startling answer to that question that might be summarized in this way: "The Church should be loving the world."

Just listen to the first line of that document: "The joys and the hopes, the griefs and the anxieties of the men of this age—especially those who are poor or in any way afflicted—these too are the joys and hopes, the griefs and anxieties of the followers of Christ."

How wonderful that is! How warm and affectionate! After centuries of much self-preoccupation, how delightful to see the Church trying to point, like John the Baptist, not to itself but to another: to the world, to the world it is meant to serve and sanctify. After generations of a certain antagonism toward the world, how startling to hear the Church beginning to sing a new song!

Today, the song our culture has us singing is the "me, me" song. It's the song that sings about how the sun revolves around me! The song the Baptist sings is "He must increase, and I must decrease." It's an invitation to point beyond ourselves and to rejoice in others, an invitation to enter into a world that revolves not around ourselves, but around Jesus its Redeemer.

In an age in which the cultural song has been leading us to a shocking lack of compassion for the needy and the most vulnerable, the Baptist invites us to sing quite a different melody! No wonder the feast of his birthday is so important that it has displaced this Ordinary Sunday of the year!

St. Peter and St. Paul

(June 29)

First Reading: Acts 12:1–11
Responsorial Psalm: 34
Second Reading: 2 Timothy 4:6–8, 17–18
Gospel: Matthew 16:13–19

❧

Today the Church celebrates the Feast of St. Peter and St. Paul, two giants of the first-century Church, martyred around the year AD 65 during the persecution of Christians by the Roman Emperor Nero.

Tradition has it that Peter was crucified, and that he asked to be crucified upside down since he felt unworthy of dying in the same way Jesus had died. Paul, although Jewish, was a Roman citizen and, as such, protected from death by crucifixion. So, Paul was beheaded around the same time Peter was crucified.

In celebrating these two pillars of the Church, it would be easy to get caught up in the heroics of their lives. To speak about their hardships as recounted in the first two readings. And to be amazed at their faith!

But faith—our own faith, and that of St. Peter and St. Paul—has less to do with being a prisoner of the state than with being a prisoner of our own fears. Faith has less to do with heroics than with ordinary, everyday living!

St. Peter and St. Paul

We are a people of faith, or we certainly would not be here! We're not giants of faith as were Peter and Paul. But we each share the same gift from God—the gift of faith that comes from beyond us.

Jesus calls Peter a Rock, but the Gospels remember him more often as clay. Peter is the one who fled into the night at Christ's trial. How different the Peter of the Gospels is from the Peter portrayed in our first reading today—who, the night before his trial, was able to sleep soundly as a prisoner in Herod's jail. What accounts for Peter's incredible transformation?

I believe the only answer is faith.

Faith changed him. God's strength surged through Peter's life to move him BEYOND HIS FEARS! And it was the same for Paul. And it's the same for all of us.

Our fears are real, and we wonder what God will ask of us. There's a wonderful verse in the second reading from Paul's Letter to Timothy. Did you hear it?

Paul writes to Timothy: "The Lord stood by me and gave me strength."

This is a key message of the New Testament: the Lord stands by us to give us strength. Peter and Paul discovered this in their moments of greatest need. So, today's feast is not as much a celebration of St. Peter and St. Paul as it is for the gift of faith that sustained and transformed them through their lives.

And Paul writes: "The Lord will continue to rescue me from every evil threat and will bring me safe to his heavenly kingdom. To him be glory forever and ever. Amen."

THE TRANSFIGURATION
(August 6)

First Reading: Daniel 7:9–10, 13–14
Responsorial Psalm: 97
Second Reading: 2 Peter 1:16–19
Gospel: Matthew 17:1–9 or Mark 9:2–10 or Luke 9:28b–36

❧

There were many mountaintop experiences in the life of Jesus. The Gospel writers say he loved to retreat to the mountains for prayer. Here, today, Jesus and his inner circle, Peter, James, and John go up on a mountain for a prayer and meditation session. And suddenly the disciples see the face of Jesus begin to glow with an unearthly light, and his clothing becomes so bright they can hardly bear to look. And who should appear in conversation with him but Moses and Elijah representing the Law and the Prophets, the Hebrew Scriptures. Their presence validates for the disciples the glory of God that they see revealed in Jesus at that moment. And they're understandably awed by what they see!

Peter suggests, in a babbling sort of way, that they build three tents and hunker down there—in the hope that they could capture and make permanent this sublime experience. But suddenly a cloud overshadows them all, and a voice from the cloud speaks some of the same words heard at Jesus' baptism: "This is my Son, the beloved. Listen to him!" It was a glorious and defining moment in the life of Christ.

And then the cloud is lifted, and the shining is gone. Moses and Elijah are gone, and there's just Jesus as they've always known him, saying: "Come on, it's time to go back down the mountain and get to work." The awesome experience of the glory of God, as wonderful as it is, is not to be enshrined as a way of preserving it.

This Gospel story gives the bare bones of a peak religious experience Jesus had. And I think it has a parallel in our own lives that gives it special meaning for us.

All of us have had mountain top experiences in our lifetime that have had great importance for us. The first big adventure. The first big success. The first love. The wedding day. The first deep religious experience. The first time we felt God was real and very close, and that God cared. All these times were filled with joy and deep satisfaction. We look back and remember these peak experiences when life seemed so wonderfully fulfilled. And there's something in us that yearns for that to last. Oh, how good it is for us to be here, we say with Peter, James and John.

We look at the crest of the wave we're riding, and we say: Let's freeze the moment! We look at our family life, we look at our children, and we say: "This is the way I want it to be forever." Or we look at the spiritual high we've been on, the long stretch of consolation and strength from God, and we want this to last forever.

But of course, realism comes along and says: That's impossible. Even with the most perfect wedding day, sooner or later, there's conflict. Because you're two people, not one. And even with the best of jobs, sooner or later restlessness or monotony sets in. And even in the best prayer life, temptation and dryness and desolation come along.

The desire to stay on top of the mountain is understandable but unrealistic. Because we're meant to come down from the mountain and to embrace the uncertainties and difficulties that are part of every human life. Jesus himself had to come down the mountain— to his own dark destiny.

St. Luke, in his account of the Transfiguration, tells us that what Jesus was talking about with Moses and Elijah was the journey he was going to be making to Jerusalem. They're talking about his coming passion, suffering, and death! In the middle of that sublime event, Elijah and Moses come along and mess up the whole picture! Jesus is there in all his glory, even his clothes ablaze with light, and what these two want to talk about is his suffering and dying! What a downer!

There are some of us who are tempted to look at our Christian faith for a guarantee to a life free from trials and suffering. And when these inevitably come, we wonder where God is! Or we wonder what we've been doing wrong. How can God let us suffer so? On a much larger scale, we wonder if God has abandoned the victimized of the world. Has God forgotten the innocent people of Haifa, and Tyre, and Sidon? Great darkness is covering that part of the world these days! And it's terribly hard to find God in the darkness. Like Peter, we want to capture the glory and avoid the pain. Because we think we can find God there in the glory, but not in the darkness of human evil or of natural disasters.

I'm thinking of the July bombings in Mumbai and of the almost daily car bombings in Iraq. I'm thinking of the recent flooding in Indonesia and the wildfires in California. I'm remembering the pictures I saw this week of the bodies of children being recovered from the rubble of bombed buildings in Qana, Lebanon.

Some of us question: where is God in all this? It's the same question we asked on 9/11. And, clearly, events like these make it very hard to believe that God loves us and has our best interests at heart. It's terribly hard to find God in the darkness of human and random evil.

It will be very hard for Peter, James, and John to find God as they accompany Jesus into the darkness of Gethsemane, or as they learn about his passion and death the next day. What happens on the mountain top in this Gospel scene today is preparation for what will happen at Gethsemane and Calvary. The mountain top is a kind of preemptive strike against Good Friday. Jesus wants them to remember that experience on the mountain top and to let it strengthen them for the scandal of the cross. The high of the Transfiguration is for all the lows that lie ahead of them.

There's a lesson for us here. And it's this: We must learn to trust God in the darkness. Christian faith is essentially that. We trust in God's goodness and power and love, even when God seems to be conspicuous by his absence. This is the attitude of one of the great heroes of the Old Testament, Job. When he's faced with multiple disasters, one after the other, his temptation is to denounce God altogether. Instead, Job speaks these words—words that may be the greatest words of faith recorded in the whole bible: "Though he slay me, yet will I trust him."

"Though he slay me, yet will I trust him" (Job 13:15, NKJV). That's faith at its purest. And it's what all our mountain top experiences are preparing us for.

THE EXALTATION OF THE CROSS
(September 14)

First Reading: Numbers 21:4b–9
Responsorial Psalm: 78
Second Reading: Philippians 2:6–11
Gospel: John 3:13–17

I suspect some of you may be wondering what this feast of the Lord is all about today, and how it happens to show up on a Sunday! It's not often that a feast day gets to replace the regular Sunday readings and prayers. Today's Feast of the Exaltation of the Cross has had greater prominence ever since the Second Vatican Council because it turns our attention to the central mystery of our faith— to the death and resurrection of Jesus at a time when the Easter Season may be just a dim memory. It brings a touch of April into September!

The cross the liturgy speaks about today is the cross Jesus carried and died on, not the cross any one of us or any of our friends or family members may be carrying. Those crosses, as well, receive a lot of attention in the New Testament. In fact, just two Sundays ago we heard Jesus say to his disciples (and that includes you and me!): "Whoever wishes to come after me must deny himself, take up his cross, and follow me" (Matthew 16:24). Not one of our favorite sayings of Jesus, I'm sure!

Who wants a cross? Who needs it? We react to it with fear and flinching. But the fact is life gives them to you. We don't have to go looking for them. It might be a sudden illness, or a difficult family relationship, or a dead-end job, or a wretched temper that makes you snap at your best friends.

Whatever we find painful and hard to put up with qualifies as a cross in our lives…especially the sufferings we have to endure in order to do the right thing! That is, in order to do the Christian thing—which so often is in opposition to what the secular world is preaching and doing.

But the sufferings you and I may have to endure are minor compared to the suffering of most people in the world today. We see graphic images of that suffering on our TV screens and in our newspapers every day. And that suffering seems to be multiplying!

To speak about our human sufferings this morning would be off topic for today's feast. Suffice it to say that God does not desire suffering—in any form! God did not demand Christ's suffering and does not want ours. God works to overcome suffering! We see that so clearly in all the Gospels where Jesus was utterly dedicated to the healing of suffering.

This morning, we want to look at his suffering, at his cross. And an indispensable help to that is the second Scripture reading from St. Paul's Letter to the Philippians. Paul writes that God the Son, the second person of the Trinity, "did not regard equality with God the Father something to be grasped. Rather he emptied himself, coming in human likeness." He emptied himself!

That self-emptying was total. In becoming one of us, God the Son kept nothing back for himself. No divine privilege that might have preserved him from torturous suffering and a horrible death.

None of the power and position and glory that comes with being equal with God the Father and God the Holy Spirit. He never stopped being God, but he freely and fully surrendered all the powers of God and spent the rest of his life dependent on his Father's will, as each of us must be.

In his last moments on the cross, Jesus surrenders the only thing he had left to give—his grasp on his own humanity. "It is finished" (John 19:30). I have nothing left to give. He was emptying himself once again, just as at the Incarnation.

Paul says that Jesus wasn't coerced into this decision. He took it on freely and accepted the full consequences of becoming fully human and of being faithful to his Father's will.

That fidelity to his Father's will of bringing "God's kingdom to earth as it is in heaven" inevitably brought him into conflict with the powerful political and religious people of his day. And in such a conflict he was—humanly speaking—bound to lose. Human power and malice made his suffering and death inevitable. Any astute analyst of first-century Palestine would reach that conclusion.

He did not want to be crucified. You remember how St. Luke, in his Gospel, describes Jesus as he prayed in the Garden of Gethsemane to be delivered from the death awaiting him.

Luke writes that in his anguish, his sweat fell to the ground like great "drops of blood" (cf. Luke 22:44). And Jesus prayed: "Father, if you are willing, take this cup away from me; still, not my will but yours be done" (Luke 22:42). Clearly, the cross was not something he chose for himself. What he chose was to be faithful to his human condition, to his own humanity, and to being the human face of God on earth.

So, this feast today is a reminder to us that when we look at a crucifix, what we're seeing is an icon of divine solidarity with our pain and our problems. This is God the Son hanging on that cross and suffering with me! Not a detached, uninvolved God—observing my pain from afar.

Death on the cross was not the end of the story, of course. Two days later, Jesus is raised, and the cross that had been the instrument of torture and death is now glorified and exalted. It's glorified and exalted because it shows us that nothing is beyond God's life-giving reach: no failure, no suffering, no disappointment, and no death in any shape.

This deserves an Easter's Alleluia this morning!

THE COMMEMORATION OF ALL THE FAITHFUL DEPARTED (ALL SOULS)
(November 2)

First Reading: Wisdom 3:1–9 or Isaiah 25:6–9
Responsorial Psalm: 23
Second Reading: Romans 5:5–11 or 6:3–9 or 1 Corinthians 15:20–28 or 15:51–57 (or multiple other options)
Gospel: John 6:37–40 or multiple other options

The feast we're celebrating today used to be known as the Feast of All Souls. Then, not too long ago, All Souls Day got a new name, "the Commemoration of all the Faithful Departed." There was a good reason for the change in name. We're remembering persons today, not just their souls! Today we're remembering all those who have gone before us in death—our family members, our loved ones, our friends, our neighbors. I don't know about you, but for me that list keeps getting longer and longer! This Sunday brings them all to mind, and that's good. It gives us an opportunity to thank God for their lives—for what they've meant to us, and for all they've given to us.

The Commemoration of All the Faithful Departed

Today is also an opportunity to reflect on death, and on what our Christian faith teaches us about death. And that's good, too. Because most of us studiously avoid thinking about death! It remains vague and abstract until someone close to us dies. And then the pain of that loss becomes like no other pain. It yearns to be consoled, and many people simply can't find that consolation. So, for Christians it becomes all the more important to know what our faith reveals to us about life after death.

What happens to us after we die? It's a question we all have and would love an answer for. Not long ago, in Catholic New York, the Archdiocesan newspaper, in the column titled The Question Box, someone wrote in and asked: "What happens to your soul when you die? One of my friends claims the soul immediately goes to heaven. Another friend says your soul remains sleeping until Jesus comes again; then we go to heaven. Can you shed any light on this?"

The answer the columnist gave was wonderful! And I want to share it with you this morning. He begins by saying we're in very uncertain and mysterious territory here. Most of the time, all we can do is speculate. Because we really don't know! God has revealed so very little about life after death.

But there are some things we do know. First of all, we know there are people in heaven right now! Jesus, first and foremost. That Jesus rose from the dead and ascended into heaven is one of the bedrocks of our faith. St. Paul goes so far as to say that if Jesus has not been raised from the dead, then our faith would have nothing in it, and we Christians would be the most pitiful people in the world! (see 1 Corinthians 15:14, 19).

We profess our faith in the resurrection of Jesus from the dead every time we say the Nicene Creed—as we'll do this morning. And we believe that, along with Jesus in heaven, there are the countless number of people we commemorated yesterday—the Feast of All Saints—the greatest of them, of course, being Mary, the mother of Jesus. So, we know there are people in heaven! "Today you will be with me in paradise," Jesus tells the good thief crucified alongside him (Luke 23:43).

A second thing we know is that after death there is no "time" as we have it here (hours, days, years) and so on. Time-related words like *before, after, during*—such words are meaningless when we're speaking about eternity. With God there is no past or future, no yesterdays or tomorrows. For God, all that is, exists in one eternally present moment—in one NOW. That's what we mean by "eternity." Imagine that! One eternally present now! Sometimes we get glimmers of this eternity in our own lives—when time seems to stop and stand still, when we're so caught up in whatever it is we're doing that we're blissfully unaware of time passing. Surely, you've had experiences like that.

And one other thing we know. Both our body and soul are essential for being a human person. There can never be a human soul floating around somewhere without a human body! If a soul is not existing in relation to a body, we're not talking about a human person anymore. Because a human person is body and soul! That's what makes us different from the angels who are pure spirits, pure souls without bodies. A good reason for the Church to move away from calling today the Feast of All Souls is because human souls without bodies just don't make much sense.

So again, to the question: what happens to us when we die? We don't know for sure. Scripture is strangely agnostic about what's waiting for us after death. And because we can't even imagine what life after death is like, we have lots and lots of trouble believing it! So, here's an analogy that perhaps may help.

Consider for a moment the life of a fetus in the womb. When we're within our mothers' wombs, all our needs are met. We feel warm and secure, and we're being fed. We're quite comfortable with the life we know.

And if anyone were to tell us about the trauma of birth, and about our entry into the world, we would choose (if we could) to stay in the womb. Right? But now that we know life outside the womb, who of us would trade it for a womb existence? I think there's a parallel here for our lives after death.

Even though we don't know for sure what happens at death, even though we don't know what life after death will be like, we can believe. We can trust that the same God who knit us together in our mother's womb, and who brought us into this life, will continue to care for us in the transition from this life to the new life of eternity.

So, here's the explanation that the columnist in Catholic New York gives for that question sent in to him.

The question again was this: "What happens to your soul when you die? One of my friends claims the soul immediately goes to heaven. Another friend says your souls remains sleeping until Jesus comes again; then we go to heaven." And the answer he gives is this:

"When we die, our next conscious moment will be the resurrection, our rising to the new life St. Paul attempts to describe in the fifteenth chapter of his First Letter to the Corinthians." And by the way, we heard a small section from this chapter of Paul in our second reading this morning. But I'm going to repeat that answer again.

I find this explanation fascinating and immensely consoling! It makes a lot of sense to me, and it concurs with all three Scripture readings this morning. "The Lord God will destroy death forever," we heard Isaiah say in our first reading.

"All of us are to be changed, in an instant, in the twinkling of an eye. The dead will be raised incorruptible, and we shall be changed," writes Paul to the Corinthians.

And Jesus, in John's Gospel from today's Gospel reading, promises: "Everyone who believes in me shall have eternal life, and I will raise him up on the last day."

Three times in a row—in quick succession—God's word to us today is pure good news! We hear Scripture texts that demand nothing from us but faith.

We're not being exhorted to be responsible today! We're not being admonished for our weakness and self-indulgence! We're not being warned to mend our ways, as we pray today for those who have gone before us in faith and as we anticipate our own dying and meeting with God.

Today, when we commemorate all our dead relatives and friends, the unknown dead, and those who became known to us only in their deaths, we can lay aside all anxiety about ourselves and about them. Instead, we commend all the dead and ourselves to the love of God in Christ Jesus. And it's for that boundless, powerful, and unimaginable love that we gather to give thanks this morning as we remember our dead who live on—body and soul—in an eternity that's beyond our capacity to imagine.

THE DEDICATION OF
JOHN LATERAN
(November 9)

First Reading: Ezekiel 47:1–2, 8–9, 12
Responsorial Psalm: 46
Second Reading: 1 Corinthians 3:9c–11, 16–17
Gospel: John 2:13–22

❧

Every once in a while, a Holy Day like the Feast of All Saints on November 1, or the Immaculate Conception on December 8, falls on a Sunday. And then the regular Sunday Mass, with its own Scripture readings and prayers, gets displaced in favor of the Mass for the Holy Day. We saw this last Sunday when we commemorated All the Faithful Departed. And we see this again today. Today's Mass is not the regular Sunday Mass. Instead, we celebrate the dedication of a particular church in Rome.

Many Catholics are surprised to find out that the cathedral church of Rome is not St. Peter's. The cathedral church of Rome, and the pope's parish church, is the Church we're honoring today —the Basilica of St. John Lateran. That's where the pope comes to celebrate Mass on important occasions during the year, and when he wants to speak especially to the people of Rome, the members

217

of his own local church. The Lateran Basilica in Rome today is not the original building. The original church was built in the fourth century AD 324 by the Roman emperor Constantine. It's been destroyed and rebuilt many times since then. And for eight hundred years, on November 9, we've been honoring the Lateran Basilica.

So today, we're singling out one important church in Rome. But in a more fundamental way, we're celebrating the Church itself, and its long history these past two thousand years. And so, I'd like to say a word about the Church itself this morning. At the risk of sounding overly simple, I'd like to remind you that the Church is the whole collection of baptized people around the world who believe that Jesus is God made human, and who try to live their lives as he taught us to live. The Church is not just the pope and the bishops. It's not just the Archdiocese of New York. And it's certainly not just a building—like this one we're in—this beautiful building of brick and mortar and stained glass. The Church can never be identified with a building! The pope and bishops of the world are an important part of the Church, and a very visible part of the Church, but they're not the Church. Because the Church is all of us—the whole motley collection of us, and not just the ordained ministers of the Church. The whole Church exists under the guidance of God, the Holy Spirit. But its members—ourselves—we're only human, and that means sinful and imperfect!

Maybe I don't even need to say this to you, but we need the Church! We need the Church even more than we may think!

We need the support of other people and the companionship of other like-minded people who are trying to live by the same standards. We need the sacraments that are available to us only through the Church. We especially need the Eucharist! The sacrament that brings Christ into our physical bodies. The bread that nourishes and brings life to us. The very presence of God as our food!

And we need the structure, and the customs—the traditions of the Church. We need the guidance we receive from bishops, and theologians, and holy people of the Church. We need them because it's very hard to find God alone!

Sometimes, you'll hear people say: "I don't need the Church. I'd rather talk to God in my heart. I can find God in my own way." I have to tell you this morning, this is very hard to do! It's very hard to find God alone! If you're a spiritual genius maybe you can do it. A genius like Mozart didn't need piano lessons to mature as an artist. But all of us need the community, and the structure, to grow spiritually.

And that's because we're social creatures! That's the way God made us. We're not made to be alone. We need one another and depend on one another for the basics in life. And God doesn't bypass that when it comes to religion and spiritual development. God doesn't set up some sort of private path for me to get to Him. We need the Church; we need to feel part of a believing and worshiping community.

And the fact that the Church has survived its two-thousand-year history, despite the schisms and heresies, despite bad popes and scandals—this is a clear sign that God is behind it, supporting it! Think of it! Two-thousand years old! No other human institution in the world today has lasted this long! By all human standards, the Church should have died long ago!

So today, as we honor a particular church in Rome that was built in the year 324, we have reason to be grateful for God's gift to us of the Church. Despite all its imperfections and all the mistakes it has made in its long history, the Church continues to be Christ's way of bringing us closer to him and of being the sign of his presence in the world.